Sales and Distribution Management

Sales and Distribution Management

(Second Edition)

U.C. Mathur
Professor and Director MDP
Integrated Academy of Management and Technology
Ghaziabad, (U.P.)

NEW AGE MANAGEMENT

An Imprint of

NEW AGE INTERNATIONAL (P) LIMITED, PUBLISHERS

New Delhi • Bangalore • Chennai • Cochin • Guwahati
Hyderabad • Kolkata • Lucknow • Mumbai
Visit us at **www.newagepublishers.com**

Published by New Age International (P) Ltd., Publishers
First Edition: 1996
Second Edition: 2012

Branches:

- 37/10, 8th Cross (Near Hanuman Temple), Azad Nagar, Chamarajpet **Bangalore**-560 018. Tel.: (080) 2675 6823, Telefax: 2675 6820 E-mail: bangalore@newagepublishers.com
- 26, Damodaran Street, T. Nagar, **Chennai**-600 017. Tel.: (044) 24353401 Telefax: 24351463, E-mail: chennai@newagepublishers.com
- CC-39/1016, Carrier Station Road, Ernakulam South, **Cochin**-682 016 Tel.: (0484) 2377004, Telefax: 4051303. E-mail:cochin@newagepublishers.com
- Hemsen Complex, Mohd. Shah Road, Paltan Bazar, Near Starline Hotel **Guwahati**-781 008. Tel.: (0361) 2513881. Telefax: 2543669 E-mail: guwahati@newagepublishers.com
- 105, 1st Floor, Madhiray Kaveri Tower, 3-2-19, Azam Jahi Road Nimboliadda **Hyderabad**-500 027. Tel.: (040) 24652456, Telefax: 24652457 E-mail:hyderabad@newagepublishers.com
- RDB Chambers (Formerly Lotus Cinema)106A, 1st Floor S.N. Banerjee Road, **Kolkata**-700 014. Tel.: (033) 22273773 Telefax: 22275247, E-mail:kolkata@newagepublishers.com
- 16-A, Jopling Road, **Lucknow**-226 001. Tel.: (0522) 2209578, 4045297 Telefax: 2204098 E-mail: lucknow@newagepublishers.com
- 142C, Victor House, Ground Floor, N.M. Joshi Marg, Lower Parel **Mumbai**-400 013. Tel.: (022) 24927869. Telefax: 24915415 E-mail: mumbai@newagepublishers.com
- 22, Golden House, Daryaganj, **New Delhi**-110 002. Tel.: (011) 23262370 23262368 Telefax: 43551305. E-mail: sales@newagepublishers.com

---

ISBN : 978-81-224-3265-7

₹ 175.00

C-11-04-5483

Printed in India at Glorious Printers, Delhi.
Typeset at In-house.

PUBLISHING FOR ONE WORLD
NEW AGE INTERNATIONAL (P) LIMITED, PUBLISHERS
4835/24, Ansari Road, Daryaganj, New Delhi-110002
Visit us at **www.newagepublishers.com**

PREFACE

The book is meant to cover the syllabus of most universities and business schools.

It should not come as a surprise to the students to know that the discipline is as old as the ancient history. Even in prehistoric times products or services were bought and sold. Selling of slaves was quite common in those days. With the passage of time its importance of sales in the world of business and commerce has increased manifold. People the world over have need waiting to be fulfilled by the sellers of certain products. From this statement the principle of demand and supply emerges. When the demand of a product increases with stagnant supply the vacuum thus created is often filled with competitive products.

Market is, therefore a great leveller of sales, profits and competitive action with its incessant and unforgiving nature, where unacceptable sales are never allowed to continue and the product itself determines its position in the market place. Product, its package, brand and terms of business normally define the ground realities and exact status of the product.

Sellers need to understand that the market is in existence from centuries and will perhaps remain forever. However, some sellers will survive the competitive nature of the market and others will just perish. It is for this precise reason that sellers need to remain on the alert all the time to cash on the opportunities coming their way in the market.

Companies operate through their functional disciplines, like production, HR, finance and marketing. In marketing of today, sales, after sales service, advertising and marketing research are the work areas. As can be seen it is only the sales function that brings in the revenue, all others only spend the money. To crystallise this point in the Petroleum industry it is said that, "the person holding the last metre of hose pipe delivering petrol in cars is the most important one as he is the only one collecting cash from the customer" in retail parlance it is the shop salesperson delivering the goods and collecting payment for the same holds the key to the company's success. And yet he is perhaps the most neglected of the lot in a business. The book has attempted to bring the person into focus along with the retail sales outlets to stress on the importance due to them.

—U.C. Mathur

CONTENTS

1

MARKET EVOLUTION—FROM SALES TO MARKETING

1.1 INTRODUCTION

In the beginning of the time, people lived in caves, hunted for food and searched for edible roots, fruits. The division of work or of labour started with more proficient hunters going for the beasts while others kept the search for vegetable foods. Next, minerals were found. The women were engaged in preparing food for eating and shaping the animal hides for wearing and using minerals as cosmetics. We can consider the women as manufacturers of that time.

Later, people found that they had a little surplus of a few items of food or clothing while they needed some others. This lead to persons going with their ware to neighbouring tribal areas to barter their products with those of the tribal areas they were visiting. These persons were the first salesmen. As the commerce increased, it became necessary for some people to precede the salesmen who could talk about the products. Thus started the profession of advertising.

Still later, the Community Heads, the Warriors and others who had nothing to sell, and yet they wanted to buy, needed an item, which they could give in exchange of goods. The currency and monetary systems can find its genesis from this point.

From such beginnings, we have reached today into the world of supermarkets, internet sales, with highly competitive products coming out in the market on a continuous basis. This has lead to organized market research into the needs of the customers, research and development for developing such products, besides other innovative products which find market eventually, like the cell phone, and with it diverse and complex distribution systems. The government of the country, its monetary systems, money supply organizations and greater awareness of products and their needs among the customers, has made the market place complex as also rewarding.

Sales management was, initially under the purview of the producers or manufacturers who went out with their produce to the market place (please recall the weekly or monthly markets or Haats prevailing till today all over India). With increase in number of producers, the supply became more than the demand for most products, resulting in the specialized discipline of salesmanship. With increase in competition, it was soon found that only glib talk of a salesman was not enough. Paying public wanted value for money. An era of quality consciousness, better packaging, branding started developing.

The sequence of market development can thus be shown as given below:

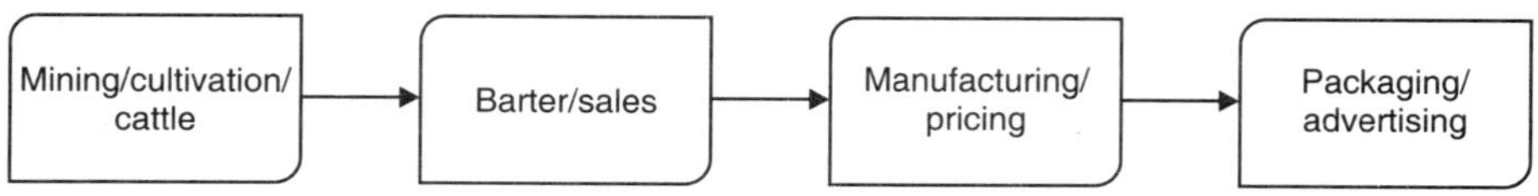

Later periods saw the burgeoning distribution channels, rise of middleman, the agency system, credit sales, and hire purchase.

Over a period of time the concept of just selling got converted into the Grand Marketing Phenomenon that may look obvious to today's student. However, the importance of sales as a discipline can never be underestimated as it is the only function that brings in the cash for the company. Production, HR, Finance, R&D are all money spenders.

Tracing back the evolution of commerce, we find that after the age of barter, beginning from last decade of nineteenth century, sales became an important discipline in business. During that time industrial revolution started in Europe followed by Mass Manufacturing Techniques –the Conveyerised Assembly Line Operation, which as per experts was propagated by Henry Ford of the Ford Motor Company. The result was increased production of Quality Goods. Hence for most products, the supply exceeded demand. It was natural, under the circumstances that the manufacturers had to resort to hard sell, or power selling techniques. Salesmanship became an extremely valued profession. Successful salesmen believed that salesmen are born and people cannot be trained to become good salesmen. And yet training for salesmanship started in right earnest at about that time, early twentieth century.

At that time, besides Salesman's profession, other areas of work opened up like that of Brokers, Sales Agents, Distributors and the Service People.

Brokers – a broker rarely handles the goods. He helps manufacturers to sell the products and for getting the orders for sale concluding the sales contract, he gets commission or brokerage from the manufacturer on the value of the contract. The manufacturer supplies the goods to the buyer, invoices the goods and collects the money. In some cases the broker could be involved in getting the payments on behalf of the manufacturer depending on the agreement between the broker and the manufacturer.

Agents – are the people, who act on behalf of some other person, like on behalf of the manufacturers. In trade there are several types of agents, like:

- Selling agents
- Commission agents
- Consignment agents
- Advertising agents
- Forwarding agents
- Buying agents
- Collection agents
- Credit enquiry agents.

Changing scenario in the twenty-first century for India:

- Opening of country's economy
- Global competition
- Better quality products
- A large variety of models of same products
- High-tech products
- New channels of distribution
- New channels/media for advertising
- Educated well informed customers, who are aware of their rights
- Complaint redress forums.

In 1991, Government of India changed the rules of the business game as follows:

- Removal of license to manufacture for most products
- Foreign equity allowed in industries
- Lower rates of import duty
- Partial convertibility of rupee
- Lowering of importance of government/public sector business.

The above resulted in several global players getting in to the country with massive investments. Later changes in governments let to slowing down of economy and reforms and in many cases foreign firms found that the large investments have not borne the expected results e.g. Daewoo Motors. However, with a large purchase group of some twenty crore people, the foreign firms believe that they can yet make a profit by just persevering in India.

Lowering import duty has helped in exports as export related manufacturers could get their raw materials imported without any problem.

This has also helped foreign firms in getting their products for Indian market, giving Indian customer the choice of a variety of goods, of better quality.

Partial convertibility of Rupee has helped exporters in more than one way, by allowing them unrestricted imports.

Public sector or government owned firms have lost their importance over the years and now the government has put quite a few of them for disinvestments. The fact that there was a Ministry of Disinvestments in the centre shows the importance the government of India places on disinvestments.

Let us examine some of the areas the sales person of the twentieth century has to cover, either singly or as a team. The following give an idea of the activities connected with the sales persons:

- **Order Taker:** The role of order taker for the sales person is age old conventional. In the early twentieth century the salesman (there were hardly any sales girls at that time), were carrying their ware with them to show samples to the customers and to demonstrate if the product called for the same. In fact co-passengers, while travelling in a train, mistook an oil company salesman for a masseur as he was carrying small sample bottles of lubricating oil.
- **Delivery Sales Person:** For products of mass consumption like milk, fuel the salesman carries the product in tankers and makes a sale by downloading the same at the customer's premises from his containers.
- **Sales Promoter:** The person does not take orders from the customers. He only makes the customer interested in the product with the help of demonstrations and discussions. Pharmaceutical firms have these types of Medical supervisors who meet with the doctors with product literature and samples and tries to convince the doctor to prescribe the medicine.
- **Technical Sales Person:** He is usually an engineer who has proficiency in optimizing the usage of the product and he works with the customers engineers as their technical support person.
- **Demand Manager:** The sales person is required to create demand by concept selling, demonstrations and product promotions
- **Solution Giver:** Has the answers to customer's problems. He works like an applications laboratory whose job is to tackle live problems and provide answers. He is a big aid to the order taker salesman.
- **Overseas Salesman:** Who handles international business for the firm. His main job is to sell the country first and bring India's Brand Equity on the top, before he can sell his products.

1.2 BUSINESS SCENARIO IN INDIA

While the Industrial Revolution had started in Europe in the eighteenth century it did not touch India till the period after country's independence in 1947. After 1947, the first Prime Minister Pandit Jawaharlal Nehru and the Government of India made the country a socialist republic, with emphasis on government's role in business and industry. A large number of public sector undertakings were formed with government funding and management. Private sector companies were considered as dishonest and therefore there was a lot of government control with license and permit Raj. Without the approval of the government officers, the private entrepreneur could not do any business. This lead to rampant corruption and bribery as a means of getting things done speedily in the government offices. A new breed of Power Brokers emerged as go-betweens between business and the government. The only concession to private business was for the small scale sector. Business suffered as the public sector firms could not bring about the needed economic growth and private sector was already handicapped.

There were a few exceptions though, like the Bajaj group, the Reliance group, who forged ahead despite the hurdles. The early big names of Tata, Birla, Modi, Singhania, Bangur, to name a few, kept the struggle going.

It was only in 1991, that the government found itself on the back foot with regard to its Foreign Exchange reserves, which had reached an all time low. On the request of the government of India, the World Bank and IMF agreed to provide loans on the condition that India opens its business boundaries to international players. This resulted in the economic reforms stated above. Now the present scene in India can be described as follows:

- A good number of MNC's have started operating in the country.
- Some Indian business have got foreign technology and finance.
- Market growth has slowed down world wide and more so in India.
- Stock market has been giving shocks with fluctuations and scams.
- Terrorists have further down swept the market.
- Advertising and almost continuous promotion has become omnipresent.
- Job market has slowed down both in India and elsewhere.
- IT Industry has had a set back.
- Lot of firms are busy in down sizing/right sizing their operations.

What the future holds is difficult to predict. One thing, which can be said with certainty, is that while specialists will give way to generalists, innovation and quality will play a vital role in the success of any firm.

India is a vast country with lots of diversities. Punjab and Andhra are known as the granaries of India. Farm labour during harvesting season migrates to Punjab from Bihar. Bihar is a rich state in minerals including iron and coal. It boasts of large steel plants and yet it has remained largely underdeveloped. Youths have taken to guns and there are a lot of Mafia gangs operating in Bihar. West Bengal and Kerala have had Marxist influence. West Bengal has suffered from labour unrest resulting in migration of industries from there, which was, at a time the industrial capital of the country. Kerala has the highest literacy rate in the country. Uttar Pradesh, Bihar and Madhya Pradesh were three largest states and now they have been bifurcated. Hopefully, this will help them in becoming better managed. Mumbai has emerged as the commercial capital and Bangalore as the IT capital of the country. Bangalore is a cosmopolitan city with good climate throughout the year.

India has large disparities as far as personal incomes are concerned. More than seventy percent of population lives in villages, with farming as their source of income. With increase in population the land size per family gets smaller ever so often, resulting in migration from villages to towns. Metros like Delhi and Mumbai population increase has taken its toll on the civic services, which keep crumbling. With better health facilities, average age has increased and now India has a large population of senior citizens. Teen population has also increased with improved health care.

India has seen social evolution of women who are now taking active part in various activities. They can be seen in offices, politics, and defence services, practically in each sphere of human endeavour.

A good businessperson needs to keep a close watch over these happenings to trace business opportunities, as newer products are needed now with innovative ideas, better distribution and customer communication

Indian business suffers from lack of awareness among international community about the quality of its products. A few black sheep who got orders from overseas by sending good samples and later on down grading product quality have tarnished country's image, which needs to be redeemed. Concentrated efforts by the government and industry are required for changing the India brand image. We have many pluses like low cost labour, minerals and a large trained work force. Today Industry, Commerce and the Government are busy in trying to correct things and their effort needs to be strengthened and speeded up. Indian embassies in abroad plays a vital role in projecting the right image of the country, its products and services in the countries they operate. They can also provide inputs to Indian business about product demand patterns overseas.

To take an example, Japanese embassy in India is doing a great job in helping Japanese business in locating business opportunities for Japanese firms. Besides, Japanese organization Jethro is providing the information on Indian industry. Japan also has a number of business liaison offices, which assist Japanese business in getting a foothold in India.

International business today continuous information on the following aspects for different countries:

- Business environment of the country
- Product demand projection
- Competitive forces

This calls for continuous Marketing Research, and Indian business tries to organize it as required. Besides, the Government of India needs to reassess its efforts in building India Brand Equity, for which proper planning and funding are important. These efforts will surely bring fruits and result in better International Business from India. A few years ago the Government had started such a programme and now it needs to be reactivated with greater zeal.

Besides the traditional exports from India of core products, exports, joint ventures for other products need to be planned. India has a large heritage of ethnic goods, labour oriented products, which need to be nurtured with care. India is also rich in culture, has a large number of religious places, and other places of tourist interests. Tourist industry is still in its infancy if we compare ourselves with the total international tourism. India needs better infrastructure in terms of hotels, transportation, communication and entertainment to attract tourists from the world over.

Unfortunately, India's image has been badly tarnished with the numerous scams, which have surfaced in the recent past. To an outsider, India appears to be ridden with corruption, infested with cheats and its people are supposed to be of lacking character. It is time that the people got their act together and they kept the country's interest uppermost and not their own.

Ethics in business is a must if we are to emerge as a world lead player in business and commerce as well. Our firms have been blamed for transgression in to Intellectual property rights area with availability of pirated products has become a reality. As regards advertising is concerned there exists a body, the Advertising Standards Council of India that monitors transgression by advertises and the council can ban any advertisement, which is considered as obscene or incorrect.

1.3 BUSINESS MYOPIA

Any business needs to define its purpose, its goals and objectives to become successful. Usually business is started with a visionary's zeal. The entrepreneur feels the market need of a product and plans to meet the demand. The following examples will give an idea, how a myopic vision can undermine a business:

- In Hollywood there were large studios producing a huge number of motion pictures and making tons of money, before the advent of Television in the USA. The film producers had defined their business as Producing and Distributing Motion Pictures! They were completely unprepared for the huge impact of TV, will have on the audience. Many large studios closed down, others incurred losses. Those like Warner survived because they redefined their business as the business of Entertaining and Educating People through Audio-Visual Media.

- At one time the privately owned Railways were making good profits in the USA. They had defined their business as The Business of Running a Railway. With increase in trucking services and luxury bus services, the railways started losing money. If they had redefined their business as The Business of Transporting Goods and People in the Country, they would themselves have got in to trucking and bus business to provide a consolidated transport system.

The need for a business definition and the purpose of business is therefore cannot be overemphasized.

1.4 WHAT IS OUR BUSINESS?

At every stage we have to understand our business, where we stand and where we want to be. How are we doing in key areas of our business? The following areas need to be analyzed for making an assessment about the business:

- Profit and loss
- Resource allocation
- Product's leadership position
- Profit centres
- Organizational structure

In business we convert resources and technological and market knowledge into increased economic value and thereby have a satisfied customer. It is knowledge which keeps firms afloat and lack of it makes them sink. From this premise emerges the age-old saying that the Customer Is Our Business.

Manufacturer's perception of business is his product range, the market demand, competition and his market share. He sees it as an extension of his manufacturing and selling base. After all, what he is making, he is selling to the customers who are in the market for the same product. Today, the manufacturer wants his customer to be satisfied by his product. It is accepted that the customers do not buy a product. They buy the satisfaction they derive out of the product.

Customers however, view the business as market places with several players and thousands of products, some of which may provide them with a degree of satisfaction. They do not even know the number of sellers of a particular product unless they are going to buy the same, at which time they start looking for alternate suppliers of a product. Sellers are aware of the plus points of their firm, its products and seldom look in to or even try to understand their handicaps and minus points. It is always a good idea to crosscheck their own assessment of their good and bad point areas.

With this view only the businessmen have gone from the concept of selling to that of marketing, which encompasses activities like marketing research, competitive strategies, new market planning and innovative business communications including advertising and publicity. What we have to understand is, are we only doing lip service to these words or are we only involved in the game of selling.

Existing situation is more close to the following:

1. Customer is hardly buying the product, which the seller thinks he is selling. He is buying the satisfaction, the product is providing to him. Therefore, if another product provides better satisfaction or a different type of satisfaction he will buy that product. For example, instead of buying a washing machine the customer may use the money for a trip to a hill station.
2. Hence products in direct competition are not the only one's to watch for.
3. Manufacturers and sellers have an idea of what the customer wants. The sellers soon discover how wrong they can be in their idea as the product is launched in the market.
4. Sellers keep harping on a particular quality of their product, little realizing that it could be of little use to the buyers. Detergent sellers have been showing discussions in kitty parties about whose sari is the whitest. Most times, women are not even cleaning the garments themselves and seldom wear white dresses. To move the customers in to buying decision for the firm's product, it is useful to know what the customer considers as the useful quality. Rational behaviour from the customer is another mistake that sellers make. We all as customers buy products we rarely use or buy an impulse to please some one. A lot of study has gone in to Consumer Behaviour to establish some rationality in a psychic activity. Sellers have to know the cause of irrational behaviour and adopt their strategy to suit it. Any attempt to change it, would be an exercise in futility.
5. Each seller has to focus on his product. However it must be understood that it is one of the million products out in the market. Customer is a non-caring forgetful person and brands and persons associated with the products are of least importance to him. Large

firms close down bringing a lot of problems to their stakeholders. The customer, however, is least bothered about it. This is the harsh reality, which the firms seldom accept.

6. Most firms assume that they know who are their customers. Understanding the market it should be assumed that firms are usually unaware of it and should get to know. Do you think the payer is the buyer or the person who decides is the customer? There can be firms whose customer group defies a definition. Take the case of a steel plant. Anyone wanting steel is the customer; he could be a builder, a designer, an architect, and a manufacturer among others. Capital equipment manufacturers may find it difficult to define their customers.
7. Buyers or the markets have been in existence for centuries and will remain there. Only the market demands of products keep changing. It is therefore, important for companies to understand the concept of "Product Life Cycle". Some products have enduring life cycle, while others like fashion garments, high technology products, including Computers, electronic goods have short life span.

It is therefore important to find out where the market exists. One should seek answers to questions like:

- Who wants the product?
- When does he want it?
- Where does he want it?
- What price he is willing to pay for it?
- What is the purpose for which he is buying the product?
- What does the product do for him in his life?
- What are the factors influencing the purchase?
- Who is the competitor?
- What are his plans?

For each firm, there are the following categories of customers:

- The buyers
- The non-buyers who buy competitive products
- The non-buyers who do not buy the product at all
- The non-buyers who buy the product only rarely
- The vacillators who keep shifting purchase between the firm and competition

It may be a good idea to find out how the customer is spending his discretionary income, the income (also called the disposable income), which he has left with after he has made all necessary payments. How the customer spends money and time? How are the customers trying to get satisfaction from the money they are spending? These insights will offer a clearer idea of consumer behaviour than any other type of research.

Do we know what our customers and non-customers are buying from our competition and with what satisfaction levels? Are they in competition with our products and services directly and are the satisfaction levels remaining constant or changing both for our products and those of competition? Answers to these questions will provide the required strategies for future action in terms of products and services.

As we get the answers we come to the crunch, do our present and future products likely to provide better satisfaction levels to the customers than those from the competition?

It may be a good idea to play the devil's advocate at this point. Let us ask the question, can our customers do without buying our products? Will it be economic consideration, political will or market changes which will decide on the subject? Can low priced products give way to high performance products irrespective of higher price? Do we have the capacity to meet with such and similar situations? How does the customer work out for the value and economics as compared to his satisfaction levels with different products? We have to really know our customers and prospective customers who are buying from competitors today.

It can thus be assumed that it is the knowledge about various elements of business, which is critical to the success of the firm. The knowledge is needed in the following areas:

- Own products, their plus and minus points
- Competitor's products, their plus and minus points
- Niche market, and its business potential
- Relevant customer group, the buyers, users and the purchase decision makers
- Market dynamics, changing trends in product demand.

The knowledge needs to be used for, first to understanding the market and then planning strategies for achieving leadership position in the market. The knowledge should lead to excellence in operations of the firm otherwise leadership position will remain a pipe dream only. Profits, on a continued basis result from application of the specialized knowledge by the members of the firm. Excellence in core areas like technology, marketing, finance, government liaison or human resource management is typical of all top-notch firms. The firm need not be large in size, but some core competencies will lead it to a high profit area. What the firm does well and what it does poorly are known facts to the firm and if it wishes it can make the weak areas as strong as others, with determination and will power.

Let us discuss some of the knowledge areas, which help in achieving success:

- Knowledge of own business can be easily understood as the areas of excellence within the firm. Some firms excel in marketing, others in new product development, and yet some pride themselves in the quality of their products and their operations. Knowledge of firm's core competence is important.
- Knowledge of customer needs, both specified or known and unspecified, becomes essential for business development.
- Knowledge of "the state of art technology" relevant to the firm.
- Knowledge of competition, their products, markets, technology, core competence and business methods is a must to counter competition.

It must be understood that knowledge is true only for a short period of time and it must be updated for it to remain valid and useful.

Student's Discussion Points

1. Discuss the genesis of modern day marketing. What role research plays in a company's success today?
2. A good product should automatically sell. Discuss.
3. How has the market changed over the last few decades in India?

1.5 MARKET AND MANUFACTURE

Introduction

In the beginning, the producers or manufacturers were small, they sold their wares in local areas, and once the demand for the product got established, the buyers used to throng around the manufacturers to pick up the product.

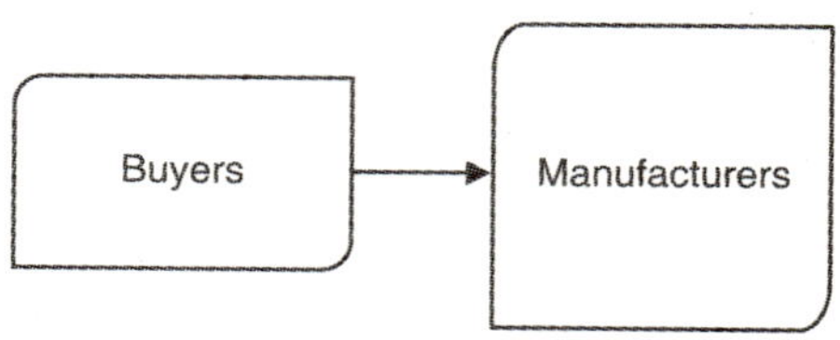

In India till the first half of twentieth century, it was totally sellers market; whatever the manufacturer produced was easily sold. The emphasis was on production and quality was not of much importance. The main reason for the situation was lack of competition and near monopoly situation for almost all the products.

Later on as the competition started seeping in to most business it became imperative that sales people coordinate with manufacturing team, to give them the idea of demand and the volumes or numbers of product which can be sold, to enable them in production planning. The stress so far stayed on manufacturing. A good firm was which had always a few more orders than the quantity, which could be produced in the given time. This put pressure on manufacturing to produce more goods, further putting the Quality on the back burner.

As manufacturing need raw materials they are buyers of the same plus they buy certain components made by others. Hence, now the picture looks as given below.

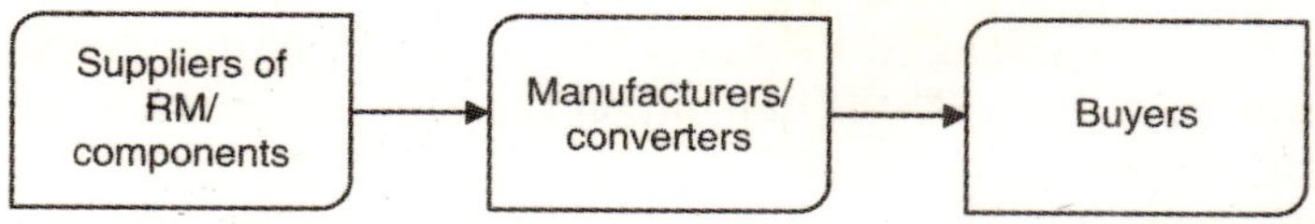

Later still people started just BUYING /SELLING and became vendors or middleman. It was from 1991, that India opened its door to foreign players and competition became a major force to reckon with by the businessmen of India.

There are the following types of products in the market:

- Consumer durables
- Fast moving consumer goods –FMCGs
- Industrial capital goods
- Industrial raw materials and components
- Industrial consumables
- Service

As for each of the product there is a distinct customer group, they need different types of selling efforts. The common factors remain as given below:

- Knowledge of market segment
- Knowledge of competition
- Business environment
- Product life cycle

Consumer durables could be as varied as cars, air conditioners, vacuum cleaners, and washing machines to computers.

- FMCGs product include soaps, shampoos plus food items.
- Industrial capital goods are the product manufacturing machines like sugar mills, textile mills.
- Raw materials are iron, steel, rubber, wood and others.
- Industrial consumables include, water, power, gasses, which consumed in the manufacturing process
- Service include the hotel industry, airlines, hospitals, insurance.

- Manufacturing units are established for making those products, which can be sold by the selling department, and therefore manufacturing and sales need to work in close coordination. In actual practice, most manufacturers are essentially assemblers of components,which they purchase.

Sales organization is designed to sell the products made by the manufacturing unit. However, it is found that once the sales set up is in place, they can sell a lot more product, which has common customers. Bata sells shoes and besides they also sell shoe polish, brushes, laces and socks as these products complement the ale of shoes. Hence manufacturing plans of firms differ quite a lot. These depend on the market situation as also on the following points:

- Plant location
- Competitive strength
- Availability of finance
- Access to raw materials
- Access to the distribution channels

When a new entrepreneur wants to set up a competitive plant, these factors provide entry barriers to him. **The success of any venture depends on the marketability of its products. Hence, it is of utmost importance that before selecting the product for manufacture and sale, thorough Marketing Research is conducted.**

Imagine a firm, which has the best of technology, location of the factory, financial resources, manpower but no market/sales. You can imagine the fate of such a firm. Sooner than later, there will be big lock on its doors and it will go in to liquidation.

Production in a one-man shop is ideal as it is **Hand Crafted** and made exactly to customer requirements. It is like tailor made suit. In such a case, the production is limited to the capacity of one person. Handicraft, expensive jewellery, and designer clothes belong to this category of products

In order to reach a large number of customers, **Mass Production Techniques** are used, like the Assembly line production. This was introduced by Henry Ford in his car-manufacturing factory and has since become the well-tested technique for large-scale manufactures.

The latest trend however is of fast changing customer needs. It is therefore necessary to have as much flexibility built in the manufacturing process as possible to take care of changing trends and demands of the customers. This is more important in areas where the rate of obsolescence is high and cost of replacing the product with other is not so high.

1.6 BRANDED AND GENERIC PRODUCTS

Most marketers want to sell branded products. Even commonplace items like wheat flour; salt and sugar have become branded products now, as branding enables the buyers to be selective in buying a particular brand only as compared to other brands. It helps sellers in highlighting the virtues of the products to catch more business. However, over a period of time even brands become generic names, as Bata is synonymous with shoes, Mobil oil with engine oil, Dalda with vanaspati ghee. Heavy advertising effort establishes the brand therefore can backfire too, if the brand gets to be accepted as a generic name rather than the brand of a firm. Care needs to be taken in this regard for avoiding such a situation.

If the manufacturer is making a product for which he has a Registered Patent under the country's Patent laws, then he can feel secure that other competing firms will not be able to use the same design in their manufacturing process and the firm can enjoy monopoly situation at least till the expiry of the Patent. However, firms should take care of getting the Patents renewed much before the expiry date to avoid any embarrassment on account of getting caught by competition that comes with a copied product. Such copies are usually a shade better and lower in cost because the firm has not spent any money in developing the same except spending on copying costs, which is also known as Reverse Engineering.

Brands: Any firm, which becomes a Market leader normally, has at least one Lead Brand. The firm tries to sell its other products under the umbrella of that brand. Sometimes, firms use the popular brand to sell other products, either bundled with it or way of promotion of lesser-known product in coordination with the main brand. Computer sellers are known for selling bundled products when they can sell slow moving products along with fast moving ones. Brand image or brand equity is perhaps one of the two most important aspects of any business the other being market share.

Once a firm has established one of its brands as a leader it diversifies to include complementary products. This helps in increasing turn over, as also profits of the firm. However, if the new products clash with the existing ones, or their quality can be suspect in the beginning, such products could do harm to the established product. It is therefore necessary to consider remaining supplier of only Specialized Products about which the firm is sure on quality and which enjoy a good brand image. Firms can also provide Quality service for these special products, which will lead them in to better and increasing Brand image/equity and profitable sales. Thus there is always a dilemma of having specialized product or generic mass-produced ones. Today, firms are trying to customize mass produced products to gain customers goodwill. For example, you can get a Maruti car from the manufacturer with customized seats.

However, nothing can take the place of good service given by the seller for the product to the customer for increasing business and thereby increasing profits. Availability of reliable service and genuine spare parts can surely increase business as these ensure longer usage of the product, which make them cost effective to the buyers.

Today in most consumer products, which are not health related, there are three-quality categories:

1. Top quality, for the rich and discerning buyers, sold through Super markets and boutiques
2. Second Quality for the middle income buyers sold through utility stores and bargain counters
3. Third Quality for the working class buyers sold through bargain stores and small shops

In case of health related and food products, there are Government regulations, which control the quality standards of the products.

As can be seen, manufacturing function is meant to create a product, which can be used by the buyers. It therefore, becomes a conversion process, as there are a number of sub-products or components and raw materials, which go in to the manufacture of any product. Home cooking is a good example of food manufacture. The cook buys meat, vegetables, cooking oil, condiments and stoves and then he goes through a process to convert the ingredients in to edible food. It is difficult to imagine any one person who can grow his own vegetables, keep his poultry and manufacture stove for cooking. Cooking therefore is a conversion process.

As there are many other manufacturers in each area, it is important that manufacturer keeps his cost of manufacture as low as possible without compromising on his quality standards.

Quality Standards: Firms, through market surveys find out the correct specification of the product they plan to make. These specifications are then converted to manufacturing standards and firms have to keep meeting these specifications for each unit produced by them. For exporting to Europe and other places, the foreign buyers now want that Indian firms follow ISO 9000 STANDARDS. These standards help firms in maintaining their specifications and assist in tracing causes of deviations if there are any. These standards are meant to keep a check on the manufacturing process.

For Product standardization each country has its own body, mostly Government owned which defines standards for various products. While mostly it is not mandatory for firms to conform to these specifications, nevertheless it helps in product marketing to an extent to have products with these specifications.

Market Share: In order to improve market share, firms have to fight competitive forces. This can be done by different means; some of them are as follows:

- Differentiation: As customers are always looking for products, which are different from other similar products, sellers try to give a little modification in the product or service, distribution to make a marked change from the run of the mill operations. These differences should be cost effective, noticeable and acceptable to the customers.
- Cost leadership: Product manufacturing cost has a major bearing on how well it can be sold in the market. If all competitive products are equally acceptable to the customers, the firm with lower cost will gain advantage over competitors. Cost leadership is obtained by either achieving economies of scale of manufacture when the firm is able to reduce unit **fixed cost**. For reducing **variable cost,** firms have to look for experience curve.
- Quick response to market demand and needs can also provide definite competitive advantage to firms as it helps them to catch the customers with a product they are waiting for.

With increased competition, differentiation does not last long, because, competing firms catch up and COPY products are soon available in the market. These copy products are made a little better than original. Hence firms, which plan product differentiation, have to continuously keep upgrading their products. Otherwise, ME-TOO products can take a good share of market share.

Customers need to know about the firm's products. Therefore communication with them is of utmost importance. This communication takes place in the following two ways:

1. Personal meetings
2. Advertising

Since these areas of marketing are of importance, they are dealt with in separate chapters.

Task for the Students

1. Make a list of popular brands and rate them.
2. Find out differentiated products, which have been introduced in the market.

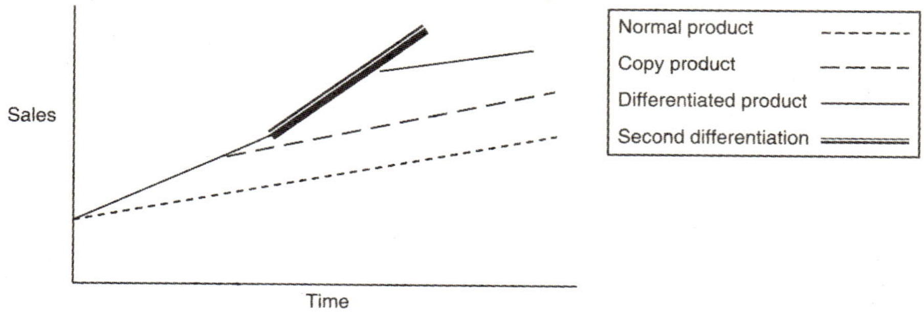

1.7 MARKETING MIX

Introduction

Business and commerce have become two important accepted activities in the life of human beings. These transcend nations, regions, cultural diversities and languages. People are engaged in business for profit and growth. It is therefore necessary to know understand how best profit and growth can be achieved. We have seen that there are the following types of products needed by buyers.

Consumer products

- Durables
- Fast moving consumer goods

Industrial products

- Capital goods-goods needed for manufacturing consumer goods
- Raw materials needed for the same
- Consumables needed for manufacturing process

Services

In each case there are some common and some different factors where selling them for profit is concerned. These are called the Marketing Mix Factors and are given below:

- Marketing research–which can be carried out for all other factors given here under
- Product
- Packaging
- Brand name, equity
- Trade mark
- Label
- Price –inclusion or exclusion of duties and taxes
- Transportation

- Distribution
- Sales promotion
- Advertising
- Retail sales and merchandizing
- Personal selling-Salesmanship
- Credit and its control
- Training of sales personnel

While product has been discussed above, let us discuss other points.

Packaging: An attractive package definitely catches the customer's eyes and it becomes an important factor especially for FMCG Products sales. It also helps in brand and product recall when the customer goes to the market to make a purchase. Packaging helps in shelf displays and shops can utilize the shelf space optimally with the right king of packaging. It is also used in advertising of the product, thus creating a TOP OF THE MIND RECALL for the product.

Brand Name: It is the most visible form of advertising, as the product gets noticed in the shops counters, show windows and shelves. Buyers can be prompted to buy once they have seen the products brand. An easily pronounced brand creates a positive memory of the product in customer's mind. Repeat advertising is used to strengthen the brand name. The value of the brand or its equity determines its usage and sales. Brand names are chosen from the following, normally:

- Manufacturer's family name–Godrej, Tata, Birla
- Town's name–Champaign
- Product use name
- Fancy name–which the manufacturer likes
- Name which is easy to pronounce

Trade Mark: Sometimes the brand name and the trademarks are the same. Trademarks are legal signs by which the products are identified. Two competing products cannot have the same trademark. Any infringement of the trademark act can be used in the court of law.

Label: The trademark or the brand name is usually placed on the package, which is called the label. Label gives, besides the brand name, the product specifications, method of use, ingredients, expiry date, date and batch of manufacture. It is mandatory by the government to give some information like the expiry date for products like food and medicines.

Price: It is perhaps the most important of the factors as it defines the buying decisions for most products. Price changes bring about changes in quantity, which is sold as higher price may limit buyers and lower price encourage them to buy the product. Most products have price elasticity of sales. However, some products do sell in certain markets irrespective of price variations, which may occur, like the high value Mercedes car. While offering price to the customers, sellers give the price in one of the following manners:

- Price includes excise duty and applicable sales tax.
- Price excludes sales tax but includes excise duty.
- Price excludes both sales tax and excise duty.
- Furthermore, the applicability of price at which location, like ex-Factory, FOR, FOB, C&F, CIF.

Transportation: Movement of goods from the manufacturers plant to the distribution system is important as, timeliness availability of goods can make sales easy. Competitive situation calls for speed and economy in movement of goods.

Distribution: Ideally, if the manufacturers can reach their customers directly without the middlemen, a lot of saving can be made as then no middlemen commission need to be paid. However, in reality, it is seldom possible and that is the reason that a large range of distribution channels are required. Some of the popular chains of distribution are given below:

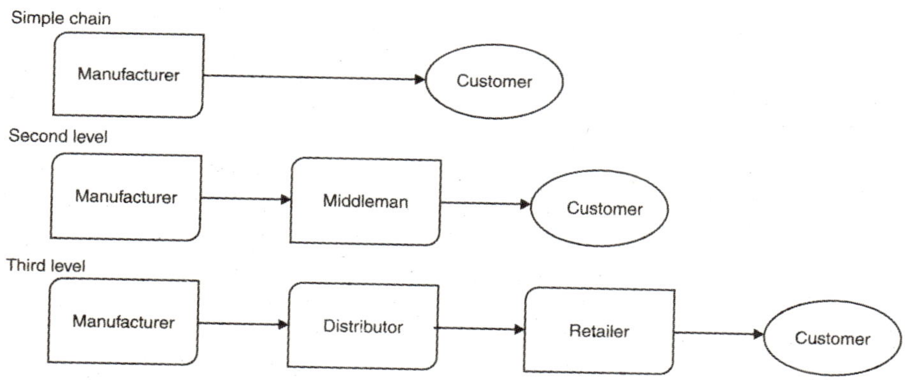

Detailed discussion on distribution, which include having firm's own shops and franchise operations are given in a separate chapter.

Sales Promotion: Sellers resort to promoting their products by offering incentives to the buyers, which makes the purchase attractive. These days we are seeing everyday that "buy two and get one free", several sellers are offering different type of incentives in a big way. These promotional offers are for both the customers and dealers or retailers. As the customers including retailers are offered an instant benefit, they are gently forced in to buying the product.

Advertising: The sellers are also trying to get customers attention on the product through non-personal communication by advertising through suitable media. In the last ten years newer media have emerged and with computer aided design facilities advertising has become more forceful and its used has spread widely. Advertising provides the customers the right to choose a product which best fulfils their needs. It is also used to combat severe competition.

Retail Sales and Merchandizing: Retail shops bring consumer products close to the customers and they fulfil a major need. In each shop there are a number of products and several brands of each product. How these are displayed and which brand gets the best place on the shelf are important areas, which help firms in increasing sales and gaining market share.

Personal Selling and Salesmanship: With the best of displays and products it is not very likely that the firm will get the eye of the customer. It is the persuasiveness of the seller or his salesman, which makes a difference. The salesman has to learn to talk the language that the customer understands best. The salesman should be able to drive home the benefits and the satisfaction so that the customer is going to derive out of the Rupee he is spending in purchasing the product.

Consider the following scene:

At a readymade garment shop the salesman is trying to sell a shirt to a customer and he says, "Sir, the shirt is made of terry silk, has good pastel shades and stud buttons" the statement is a fair description of the product.

Another salesman says, "Sir, shirt will just flow smoothly on your body as it is made of terry silk its shades go well with your complexion and matching buttons create a distinctive look" the statement catches the mind of the buyer instantly.

Credit and its Control: A credit buyer normally buys a little more because he is not paying for the product just then. It is human psychology that immunes the buyer of the thought that finally he has to make the payment and perhaps with interest. Credit can therefore be used judiciously as a sales tool with ample safeguards against fraudulent buyers.

Training of Sales Personal: As new products are introduced by the firm, new, markets emerge with increase in competition, the firm has to innovate, place new methods and structures and systems. The sales people must be therefore continuously trained in to the latest so that they keep their work optimised always.

○○○

2

Strategic Marketing

2.1 INTRODUCTION

With the changes taking place in the market place, the marketers have two choices with them, either they can be reacting to the situations or they can become proactive, on which count they have to take the initiative of planning and ***implementing*** their plans for maintaining their market share and brand equity. Today's markets are cruel and they do not forgive delays in decision-making. Strategic marketing is the key to present day market planning for the following reasons:

- Firms have to make their selections on the various strategic options
- Business environment is constantly changing, calling for timely decisions.
- Long range view is required instead of fire fighting plans.
- Strategic analysis is needed to grasp the real issues facing the markets.
- Resource allocation needs to be planned to ensure that the unfruitful tasks are eliminated from the allocations.
- Both horizontal and vertical communication and control systems should be in place.
- Strategic Marketing should help in keeping business ahead of competition during the market change phases.
- To examine the above from the Indian point of view.

Firms keep introducing new products, product variants and timing of the introduction is of strategic importance as wrong timing could meet with disastrous product launch. Wrong selection of market segment, distribution channels, pricing could lead to launch failures.

Manufacturing in India can be categorized as follows:

- Large scale
- Medium scale
- Small scale
- Cottage industry
- Cooperative sector

Besides, the differentiation can also be made as per the nature of competition as follows:

- Monopoly –where there is only one manufacturer of the product
- Oligopoly – where there are only a limited number of manufacturers say, four to six.
- Fragmented market – in which case there are a large number of manufacturers
- Section fragmented— in several products like computers, ACs there are two category of manufacturers, the branded ones and unbranded in the unrecognised or small-scale sector, with several players in each group.

Marketing strategy should be made by taking the actual ground situation considering the types of manufacturing units which are there in competition and how many of them exist.

Business environment can be categorized as a/ General environment b/ Competitive environment. It is necessary to understand the business environment and the competitive situations for developing right strategies.

The next step is to analyze the situation before planning the marketing strategies. The analyses is done for two areas-

External analysis— most of the things, which the firm needs to know, are outside of it like,

1. The market, its relevant segment,
2. The customer,
3. The competitor. Environment is also outside of the firm.

Internal analysis—

1. Firms performance,
2. Its policy and plans,
3. Objectives and deviations between objectives and performance.
4. Resource allocation for achieving the objectives in future needs to be analyzed before planning marketing strategies.

Products and markets correlate as per the following matrix:

Markets	Existing Products	New Products
Present market	Market penetration	Product expansion
New market	Market expansion	Diversification of product

Similarly another matrix gives the correlation between competition and markets:

Markets	Existing Competition	New Competition
Present market	Penetration	Price wars
Market extension	Promotion plans	Price and promotion

Strategic Marketing is all about gaining Competitive Advantage on a continuous basis and finding out the strategies, which will give you such a competitive advantage. Let us call it **Strategic Competitive Advantage.** For planning strategic competitive advantage the following method is used:

- Plan business scenario, the shape and size of the market after three and five years
- Plan your market share on the basis of feasibility
- Resources including cash flow need to be utilized for maximizing the chances of achieving the objectives.
- Focus on core competencies of the firm and synergize efforts for fully exploiting them.

Core competencies of a firm are given below:

- Technology — does it give the firm its cutting edge?
- Marketing— is the firm proactive in the market place and can it take full advantage of the business potential available in the market?
- Finance— is the firm able to generate sufficient funds for growth and expansion?
- Production— can the firms cost to manufacture, including its time dimension be compared to that of competition and is the firm finding ways of reducing cost of manufacture by going in for economies of scale and experience curve?
- Human Resource —is the firms personnel geared to think and plan their each move for the benefit of the customer?
- Government relations—does the firm maintain good and healthy relation with the government and does it avoid being on loggerheads with the government all the time? Can the firm get the government approvals at short notice?

Once the firm gets the answers to these questions it is ready to take the following strategic decisions:

- Who should be considered as firm's main competitors?
- Where should the firm compete? In which markets, geographic areas, niche markets?

- How should the firm compete? On the basis of price? On quality? Superior service, availability of genuine spare parts?
- What are the areas in which information is lacking and is needed? One off marketing research is required or should there be a continuous flow of information?
- Product multiple uses should be exploited. Bundling of products can help in selling slow moving products at least to a degree.
- Firms should plan business scenario for the next three to five years taking in to consideration competitors plans, possible likely changes in business environment

Strategic marketing decisions, which need to be taken, are listed below:

- With international players coming to India, technology is going to be rapidly changing. Indian firms would do well to either invest in R&D or purchase the **Latest State of the Art** technology to keep abreast of the competition or even forge ahead of them.
- If the product is in the maturity stage of its life cycle and demand growth has stagnated, it may be necessary to go for penetrating pricing to maintain its market share or build its brand equity to the extent that it can ask for and get a higher price than competition. Price sensitivity of the market needs to be understood and decision on pricing taken accordingly.
- If new entrants are likely to enter the market with better product, technology and brand image, it is required to invest in the product and the market by extra discounts, increased coverage and if possible, joining hands with a technology leader of the product.
- The **Customers of Tomorrow** are looking for i/ product performance improvement, ii/ product technical superiority iii/ easy availability of the product iv/ financial assistance like leasing,
- Firms should have correct idea about the benefits that the customers are seeking from the product, as it should be understood that no one buys a product, the customers buy only the benefits, which they get from the product.

Companies have understood the value of having a strong Brand equity for getting and retaining customers, as given below-

2.2 BRAND PLANS

When companies introduce a new product, they start with an initial Unique Selling Preposition, the USP, which gives the product the required boost

in the market place. However, over a period of time, other competitive firms catch on the USP, and depending on the market size, profit margins, ease of obtain the manufacturing technology and the requisite finance, they place their own products in the market. Thus, the USP of the company's product is lost as there are other products, in the market, the **"me too"** products with perhaps better USPs. In such an event, which is an almost daily occurrence, the thing, which keeps the company's product on the top, is the Brand. The brand, if projected well in the right market segment will carve a niche for itself in the mindset of the buyers with its emotional appeal.

Brands can become effective tools of differentiating products as they keep creating goodwill and become company's assets. A good brand price fixation becomes easier as higher price can be charged over the price of competitive products.

There are, however, discount stores with self-service facilities where the customers buy products at low costs and price is the main criteria with the customers. In such stores brand ceases to have a major selling point. Most retail shops sell several brands of any product. In such shops it is either the advertising pull, inventory push that makes the shop salesperson promote the sale of a particular brand or it could be the extra discount offered by one company or its distributor to the shop.

Brands have given a major fillip to customer buying habits. Customers are known to love some brands and are ready to swear by them. These customers take on themselves the role of brand advertisers or even brand ambassadors.

Brand can be defined as **"A unique name for a product of a particular manu- facturer."** This unique name gives a large number of attributes to the product and the company marketing it. As such, along with the market share, brand equity is considered as the most valuable possessions of a company.

Brand, its uniqueness, its value or equity, brand building, have become extremely important areas that need constant attention of the top management of the firms. Brand building is an evolutionary process as it takes a lot of time before a company can have strong brand equity.

In case of most products, after the initial sales starts declining due to fading of its novelty, it is its emotional appeal that helps it to sell. This emotional appeal or bonding comes from the appreciation of the brand by the buyers. Therefore, brand, its value or equity and its attraction for the buyers are perhaps the most valued properties, or assets of a company. There are a number of ways of promoting the brands emotional appeal among the buyers and these will be discussed in detail in the coming chapters.

Brand is the most valued possession of a company. Take Maruti from the car and what have you got? Brand gives a product its separate identity, taking it away from other run-of-the-mill products. Companies increase their market share and profits on the basis of strength of the brand, brand image or brand equity. It helps companies as once the buyers establish the brands through the quality acceptance. The brand equity is further strengthened with continued advertising efforts.

Jaishree Sunder of Lintas says, "At the end of the day, brands are but promises packaged with emotion. The stronger the emotional bonding, the greater the probability a brand will have of accessing additional revenue streams".

It can therefore be summarized that as the products get branded, they get the emotional appeal, in most cases and the advertiser do well to use the emotional appeal while advertising the product with its brand.

Giving brand management the importance it deserves, companies have stated modifying their marketing department's structure a given below:

First Level Structure

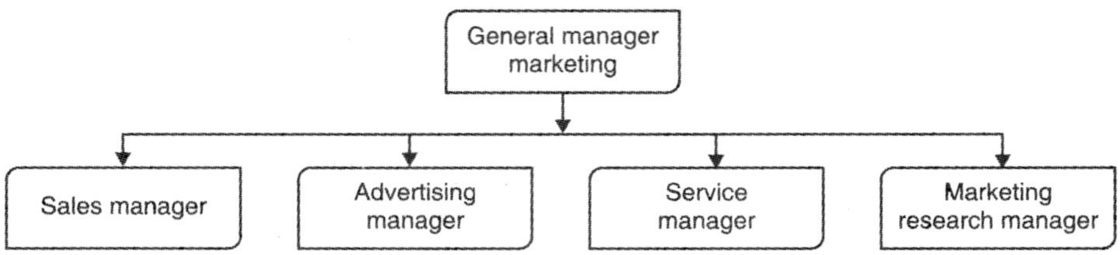

In the structure given above, the task of managing the brand is left to the Advertising Manager. With the growing importance of brand management, the structure has been modified in several companies as given below, as second level structure:

Second Level Structure

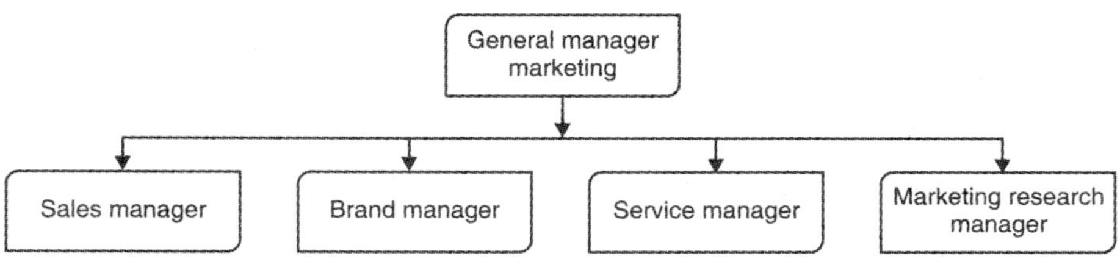

In certain companies there are several brands of one product like the Lever Brothers, or Hindustan Lever in India. There would be about eight brands of soaps, three of tea and hence they have Category managers looking after the category of soaps, tea, while they have brand managers working with item who look after individual brands as can be seen in the chart given below:

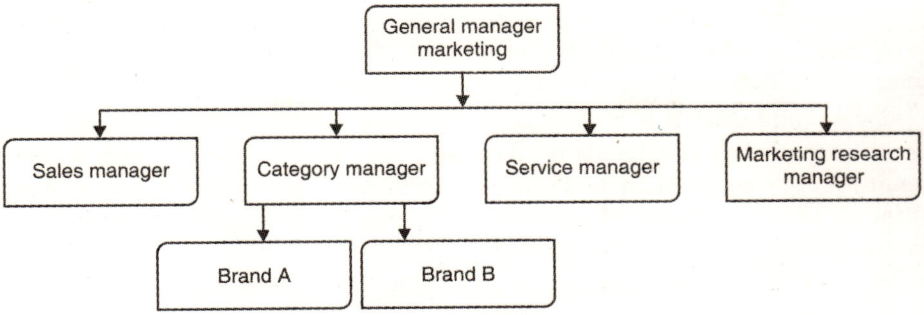

Brand manager in some companies operates like the virtual CEO for the brand he sells. He gets involved in product development process, finding out the market demand of the same, in differentiating one or all the marketing Ps. The sellers have accepted the usefulness of having brands and that is why even usually generic product like wheat flour, salt, and sugar, porridge have become branded products.

Packaging has gone a long way into making brands common and interesting as they act as advertising media as well. Packaging of FMCGs started in the late nineteenth century in the US, when companies started selling packaged goods under brand names. Prior to that time, only generic products were being sold mostly in bulk without packaging. In 1880s soaps were first, to be branded and the following brands followed soon after:

- Pears Colgate
- Royal Baking Powder
- Quaker Oats
- Regal shoes
- Waterman pens
- Coca cola

After the Ist World War, the advertising business got a big boost because peace had descended on the world business, trade and commerce started thriving again and competition started showing its head that led the companies resorting to advertising to remain in the public eye for beating the competition.

Companies stared looking towards the customers to know, with the help of marketing research, what appeals to them more than anything else. Advertisers began developing persuasive techniques and decided that the following were needed to touch the customers' psyche. Brands became useful as they started symbolizing the products. In order to make brands legal entities, companies started getting trade marks registered with their government bodies for protection against competitors stealing the brands. Trademarks are projected through words, symbols and styles used for placing these together on the product for easy identification as well as for in-built advertising affect, the brands and the trademarks have.

Incidentally, the economic value of intellectual properties is also protected by law along with the patents that are given for a product manufacturing techniques, its design and usage.

Companies have to understand the ways, methods, ideas that attract the customers; what appeals to them and then decide the best persuasive technique to be used in business communications with the customers through advertising or through personal contacts, for this the company has to answer the questions given below-

1. How can they get the job done using the product with less money but with equal efficiency?
2. How can they do a better job using the product and claim the bosses' approval?
3. Is there seasonality of demand for the product in order that they use the right time for using their persuasion strategy?
4. How can they make their brands more popular than the competitive brands?
5. How can they stressfully inform the customers about the benefits of the products for them?
6. Does the product help the customers in increasing their comfort levels; improve their appearance or their health so that emphasis can be made on these points in the advertising campaigns.

In this connection Maslow brought his hierarchy of needs theory given below:

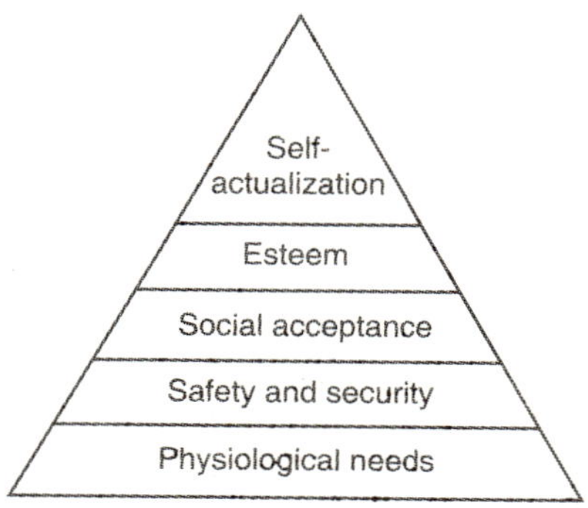

As the seller understands the hierarchy of human needs, he can plan the product communication according to the level of hierarchy he wants to satisfy with his product. For example, a basic food seller would talk about its nutritional value, calorie count for the weight conscious people. Cosmetic sellers would convey to his customer group about the beauty, allure and hope the products can provide to the users. Car sellers would give the concept of life style associated with the car, besides the comfort, excitement, thrill it would provide rather than just talking about its use a mode of transport.

2.3 THE BENEFIT STORY

The sellers must understand that no body buys a product; people buy the benefits the products provide to them. For example, a shirt seller knows that the shirts are made of terry-silk and are available in a number of pastel shades. However, if he conveys to the customer the manner in which the shirt cloth would just flow on the buyer's body and that the shades, at least some of them would go well with the buyer's complexion and physique. Given below is a table that corresponds with the Maruti Esteem's features as they could be conveyed to the buyers.

Maruti Esteem Car

Feature	Benefits
Powerful engine	Comfort and thrill
Good leg and head room	Comfort
Automatic windows	Comfort and life style
Powerful air conditioning	Comfort and prestige
Good music system	Comfort and prestige
Aerodynamic styling	Thrill of speed and lifestyle
Strong body	Safety
Seat belts	Safety
Countrywide service facility	Peace of mind

From the above given analysis it can be concluded that it is a luxurious family car. The car advertisement showing the birthday episode uses this sequence of thinking as the advertisement is planned. In the advertisement,

For creating a benefit story, the following areas need to be understood:

1. Creativity of minds
2. Standards of decency
3. Limits of the media that would carry the message
4. Legal restrictions
5. Reputation of the company

In the game of advertisement brand plays a major role as it denotes the following:

1. Standards of product quality
2. Reliability of the product, the sellers
3. Value for money being spent by the customer for buying the product
4. Trademark that conveys the authenticity of the product

Historically branding was carried out with the help of a hot ion on cattle as a proof of ownership in the 2000 BC in Egypt. Greeks and Romans branded their prisoners up till the nineteenth century.

In the first half of the twentieth century, firms in India depend on their Goodwill, which gave them an edge over their competitors. As the number of competitors was low, the goodwill earned the firm the desired clientele. However, over the years, competition has increased manifold leading to dilution of goodwill value. Maybe the association of the word goodwill has ceased to excite the buyers leading to the emphasis on brand and its value for the buyers.

Brand power gets converted into economic value and it begins and ends with a focus on brands as corporate assets. Companies that outperform their peers and competitors in brand value creation understand this well and proactively manage their brands as they would have other key strategic assets of the company as a way of securing long-term shareholder value.

Modern day branding started in the nineteenth century when some US firms started selling packaged goods under a brand name.

In India, till a few years back most of common products like flour, sugar, milk, candles and pickles were sold in bulk unbranded. Only of late, these products have found brands and sold in packages with distinctive brands, which differentiate almost similar products being sold by competing companies.

Historically, brands have been in vogue from 2000 BC, when tribes were branding their cattle in Egypt. In the nineteenth century BC Greeks and Romans were branding their prisoners and slaves as punishment.

It was only in 1880s soaps were first introduced as branded products by Pears, Colgate. Then came the other branded products given below:

- Baking powder
- Quaker oats
- Royal shoes
- Waterman's pens
- Coca cola

After the World War one, advertising industry started to grow rapidly. With mass production techniques, assembly line operations, availability of products started exceeding the demand for the same, needing the use of persuasion techniques to sell products and each seller wanted his products to outdo other products. This became the core of the branding base by the companies, where they could promote their brands by giving the factors that appeal to the buyers. Brands were on their way to becoming the biggest assets of the firms. Therefore, there is a close bonding between brand management and advertising management.

2.4 MASLOW'S HIERARCHY OF NEEDS

As companies try to persuade their buyers into purchasing their products, they have to understand Consumer Behaviour of the customers of their designated market segment. One basic method of understanding the consumer behaviour is through Maslow's hierarchy of needs, which deals with the human urges and requirements.

The first basic need of people is physiological, that of food. Clothing, shelter and human relationship. Next, people look for a safe and secure life. After that they need to have a place in the society leading to respect in the society. Finally, people expect a place in the top echelon; want to be known as achievers. Products should therefore support people's mindsets and should focus towards their needs. They can achieve this focus better with the help of a solid well-established brand.

Companies have become aware that people needing a product for satisfaction of one or more of their needs. Cosmetics sell because people want to look good, beautiful, handsome, alluring may be better than others. One cosmetic seller advertised that he really sells hope; hope that his cosmetics will make people look so good that their mates would come running to them. Similarly, carmakers provide, prestige, comfort, besides excitement to their buyers. Cars are used to transport people from one location to other. However, luxury cars have given a new meaning to travel by car, as these have become status symbols as well.

Therefore, it can be surmised that the seller who can provide the required benefits to the buyers of his designated market segment will win the race. This requires two basic ingredients, a good product and a proper method of communicating with the target in market segment. Let us assume that the product is good. For evolving the most appropriate communication the following channels are used by the sellers-

- Personal meetings, as in a retail shop, where the salesman directly interacts with the buyers
- Advertising, where the contact is non-personal through mass media like TV, Radio, Press
- Publicity where the firm draws attention of the buyers through either word of mouth communication between buyers and prospective buyers, or through free editorial contents given in the press, may be as press notes given by sellers or suo-motto information given by the press on their own volition.

Most people, who are also buyers, are looking for the following:

- Ways of increasing their income
- Better paid jobs with improvement in prestige levels both in the company and in the society
- Job security as well as security of the family from ailments, thefts and other calamities
- Popularity in the company as well in the social circles
- Praise when due from seniors

- A comfortable life style for self and the family
- A good personality that attracts friends
- Good health

A brand gets established in the customer's mindset, through its qualities for providing benefits. However, the product idea, especially for a brand sets in through advertising efforts. Repeat exposure of brand to the customers help in getting the brand into the subliminal consciousness of the mind and at the time of purchase it gets in to the conscious state. The benefit story that deals with the special features of the product binds the brand to the product. However, over exposure can make a highly developed brand a generic brand like the case of Dalda and Mobil oil, Dalda has become almost synonymous with cooking oil and Mobil oil with car's engine oil.

Product merchandising, with the help of its brand, provides effective product exposure through availability at a place convenient to the buyer, at time, price quantity as required by the buyers for profitable sales. Merchandising helps the sellers in product placement in retail, which helps in selecting the package size, shape, colour preferred by the trade and finally the customers. The package should lend itself to proper shelf display, demanding the right noticeable size and location of the shelf. The brand plays a pivotal role in grabbing the right shelf space.

Brand has the remarkable ability of differentiating the product from its competitors. It is therefore being asserted that the Brand is **an asset** of the firm (like the goodwill of the years gone by.)

Branded products normally have fixed prices and bargaining is not a common phenomenon for branded products. Brands with high equity can claim high price as the quality assurance gets built in to the brand. From the same yardstick, brands sell more and relatively with ease in retail stores selling several brands of the same product.

However, seeing the power of brands many retail stores or store chains sell their own brands, either in addition to others or exclusively. Then there are single brand stores along with specialty stores, which stock only one type of products in several brands. Brands have given rise to increase in consumer awareness of products.

Given below are the functions that brands perform in the marketplace:

- Customers start loving the brands due to their trust in the brand, brand reliability for known results from the product usage and brands perception of its ability to provide desired satisfaction levels.
- Investors believe that brands get them higher dividends and increased share value
- Brand provides the sellers promise of product quality in the form of guaranty

- Brand (like the Harley Davidson motorcycle) get in to hearts and minds of the customers
- Brand like the goodwill becomes an economic asset of the firm
- Brand helps in building a relationship between the seller and the buyer, both the trade partners and the actual consumers
- Brand results in buyer seller collaboration in brand promotion. A satisfied, happy customer will promote the brand in his business and home circles.

Advertising media that supports brands through exposing them in the market, consider a good brand as an assets as it generates good advertising revenue for them. Coke would not have any problem while buying media for advertising. Brand links media with the customers. "Yes I saw the advertisement on Star Plus channel."

Brand develops an identity of its own, which supports and focuses the product on to the customers. Brands start living in the customer's minds. Ask any Coke addict, he would proclaim from the housetops why Coke is better than any other soft drink.

Types of Brands

There are several types of brands as given below:

1. Unknown brand: The one that has been introduced and has not yet been promoted
2. Available brand: The one which can be purchased without any problem
3. Switchable brand: In which it is easy to change the brand due to low cost like the FMCG products. You can change the brand of tooth paste every month, while it may not be convenient to change the brand of your car or even refrigerator
4. Buy brands: The ones purchased regularly
5. Never tried brands: The ones just offered in the market, or even brands not advertised enough
6. Tried and rejected brands: The ones not accepted by the market
7. Orphan brands are those, which have no takers in the market as perhaps they were introduced in the market without proper market study
8. Substitute brands: That are available in the market and are bought in the event of non-availability of the preferred brand.

2.5 BRAND FUNCTIONS

Brands perform several functions in the market place, some for the buyers and others for the sellers.

Brands functions for the buyers are given below:

1. Brands make the choice of the product easier for the buyers
2. Brands reduce the cost of product search for the buyers
3. Brands reduce the time for product search
4. Brands reduce the risk factor for the buyers, in terms of quality, quantity, guaranty, resale price, after sales service.
5. Brands add to the identity and status of the buyers-he drives a Mercedes car!

Brands help the sellers as given below:

1. Sellers cost of sales reduce, as brands almost presale the products
2. Reduce their advertising and promotion costs
3. Reduce the cost of training of sales staff
4. Sellers can charge premium or skimming prices
5. Sellers can sell the entire brand line at the skimming price
6. Brands provide an entry barrier for firms planning to enter the market with the same product
7. Brands help in increasing the firm's share value
8. Brands provide an automatic product differentiation
9. Brands help in providing the promotional plans a market focus
10. Brands help in making the advertising messages simple as the brand itself conveys most to the buyers
11. Brands help in improved market focus in the advertising media
12. Brands help sell the entire product range under one brand

Branded products are pre sold since the customer is aware of the benefits they can derive out of the products, as the brands become synonymous with the benefits. Maruti brand of cars signify reliable cars with widespread service network in the country. Lux toilet soap brand itself proclaims its quality. There can be innumerable examples of the popularity of brands that helps the product sales with relative ease.

Information about product is communicated through advertising campaigns. Promotions lead to faster decisions by the customers for buying the products as the seller offers some extra benefit during the promotion period. However, when the brand gets customers' acceptance then the need for advertising and promotion reduces to that extent.

With high brand equity, the customers want to buy the product and they ask for it by its brand name and that releases the selling pressure from the retail sales person. The companies can reduce expenses on training of the salespersons except for the customers, new to the brand.

Pricing of branded products and brand lines becomes easy as with growing demand, sellers can keep prices at relatively high level, or can charge skimming prices. It is only when competition catches up with similarly well-known and accepted brand, that the company has to look at reducing the price and going in for penetrating prices.

When a company has a brand that is well accepted and even admired by the buyers, other possible entrants in the market with same product would have to have serious consideration before they take any decision for entering the market as the good brand becomes an entry barrier for other companies planning their entry with same products, at least till some one can bring in a highly differentiated product with better benefits and yet reasonably priced.

A well accepted brand requires less efforts in increasing the company's market share for the product as with the word of mouth publicity, large number of non-customers start buying the product.

A good brand is at times enough to differentiate the product from other products in the market in the same category. This differentiation further helps in increasing the product sales, that helps the company to achieve economies of scale, further reducing the production costs makes the product more saleable.

Brand becomes the advertising media in retail stores and therefore it can significantly reduce the required impact of advertising and promotion for the product.

A good brand that becomes the umbrella brand helps to sell the entire range of products sold under the umbrella.

2.6 PRODUCT RELATED ANALYSIS

It is important to know the product on offer fully, its detailed specifications—both static and dynamic as also the following:

- Who are the users of the product, how they buy it, where they buy it, how they buy it and for how much?
- How the customers use the product? Does it have a single use or multiple usages? How often they use it?
- What are the benefits, the customers are looking for in the product? Manufacturers may have a view of these benefits while the customers may have an entirely different notion of what they want. The sellers of washing powder are all talking of the whiteness of the wash, where the customers never talk about the whiteness as the reason for their buying a particular detergent powder. The best way to find out about the benefits the customers are wanting in the product is to arrange a market research in the desired market segment.

- Product pricing is an important aspect of marketing strategy. When a new product is launched and there is no competition, sellers go for skimming price, in other words they keep the price high to get the maximum profits before competition starts and they are forced by it to reduce the prices. If the sellers are looking for increasing market share they put penetrating prices, low prices to attract large customer groups. It is important to know if the products sales are affected by changes in price, i.e., price sensitivity of the product must be known by research.
- Knowledge about competition is needed on a continuous basis as regularly new competition keeps increasing and the existing competition keeps changing their plans and policies. It is necessary to know competitors 4 Ps with the knowledge updated regularly.
- Brand loyalty/equity of products, the firms and those of competitors should be well, assessed, as it is this single most important factor, responsible for market share.
- Market survey is required to find out the rate of product need in different market segments. Which segment has highest percent demand of the product and which segments follow the demand pattern. Sub-segments, niche segments and crossover segments demand must be assessed. Only after this knowledge the seller can decide about the segments he should enter or should he plan for sale in niche market.

The airline industry has found that they have basically two types of customers as given below:

1. Business-customers of this class want an air service which is, reliable, on schedule, with wide body aircrafts, easy to use airports with comfortable lounges, frequent flier programs, telephone check-ins, variety of connections and in-flight entertainment. Possible upgrades from business class to first class.
2. Tourists-look for low price travel, required schedules and several stopovers. For the sake of low price they do not mind night travels also. They look for package deals in which air tickets and hotel accommodations are all included.

Such details can only be found out by getting proper market research done.

Competitive Analysis

Next let us look at the analysis to be done for the competitors. The firm must know who are its competitors. There are direct and indirect competitors for most of the firms. The study of competitors is most useful if it is done with the customer-based approach. Once the firm has identified its direct competitors in the first instant, it is useful to evaluate **each of the competitors** on the following parameters:

- What are their business goals and objectives?
- What is the commitment level of the managers and stakeholders of the firms in competition?
- How do the managers of the firm view its growth prospects? Have they at any time considered its closure? What are the barriers to its exiting from the business?
- What is its cost structure, financial structure, cash flow position, assets and liabilities?
- How its suppliers, financiers and distribution system view the firm?
- What is its track record of meeting its financial commitments and other obligations?
- Are their product specifications in line with Indian standards? Can they meet world standards or not?
- How are their international business dealings? Are they importing and exporting or are they having only one of the two?
- Where have they positioned their product, is it up-market or for the masses? Is the product pricing in line with their product positioning?
- Are their advertising and promotional efforts congruent with their product positioning?
- How is the firm's Public Relations effort rated?
- How is the firm's Brand Equity rated?
- What are the firm's core competencies?
- What are the firm's strengths and weaknesses?
- What are the firms unmet needs as far as the customers are concerned? Unmet needs are because of, a/ customers dissatisfaction of the product, b/ customers problems. There are unmet needs of which the customer is aware and there are some of which the customers may not be even aware. Competitors take advantage by advertising their own met needs and firms unmet needs of the customers.

It is useful to do a SWOT Analysis at this stage for each of the competitors.

To sum up the following is the table for different types of analysis:

Market Analysis	Firm's Analysis	Competitive Analysis	Competitive Analysis
1. Size of the market	1. Level of customer satisfaction	1. Sales performance	9. Capacity /its utilization
2. Growth prospects	2. Brand loyalty	2. Market share	10. Product-wise market share
3. Profitability	3. Product quality	3. Brand equity status	11. Segmentwise sales
4. Cost structure	4. Service quality	4. Objectives/goals	12. Channels/sales force
5. Channels	5. Brand association	5. Marketing strategies	13. Advertising/promotion
6. Trends	6. Relative costs	6. Organizational culture	14. Reaction time
7. Key success factors	7. New product activities	7. Cost structure	15. Experience curve/exit barriers
	8. Managers capabilities and performance	8. Strengths and weaknesses	16. Value chain

Once the systems are put in place these activities mentioned in the table become automatic and they do not take much time, while they do provide the vital information for making strategic marketing decisions.

For example, the capabilities of a firm could include its financial strength; marketing base and its constraints that could be lack of motivation in the personnel. The analysis should take the Core Competencies into account.

Strategic Marketing Planning Process

Let us understand the formal process needed for planning marketing strategies in today's competitive age. Plans made should be a/ short term b/ long term. Most firms make annual plans, which are divided into quarterly plans. To be entirely market proactive, the plans should be kept flexible to enable firms to alter them to dovetail the changing market environment. The following steps are needed for making the plans:

- Analysis of External Environment
- Study of the Firms Internal Strengths and Weaknesses
- Idea Generation for Planning
- Brainstorming for Prioritizing the Ideas Generated
- Customer Behaviour Analysis
- Competitors Analysis
- Market Analysis
- Draft Annual and Short Term Plan
- Final Plans with Forecasting of Sales and Cash Flow

Customer's Analysis

We have discussed earlier why, how, where, when and how much the customers buy, which can be ascertained with a degree of accuracy through market research. Let us take a simple **Customer Behaviour** pattern. It includes the following elements of internal information processing, guided by external information and stimuli. -

- **Belief:** It is the customer's conviction and firm opinion of a product/brand.
- **Perception:** It comes from a customer's product recognition as a desirable product based on his intuition and information gathered on sensory plane.
- **Attitude:** It is the customer's way of thinking about the product, his firm opinion about it.
- **Preference:** Out of his belief, perception and attitude, the customer makes his preference of one product over other products, and tries to buy it.

Thus we can define the Multi-attribute Decision Making process as, "based on concepts of BELIEFS, ATTITUDES, PERCEPTIONS and PREFERENCES" which is the notion that objects in a choice set can led to external behaviour. Each object in the set has a value on each attribute used to define the choice set.

Let us take an example to illustrate the point. The purchase of a car in a family is a major event and decision-making process is multi-dimensional one. While film stars buy the car as a status symbol, middle class persons buy it as a means of transport only. Let us take four cars in the economy segment and plot their benefits to the customer. (The figures given in the table are only arbitrary and not conclusive)

Benefits	Zen	Santro	Matiz
Comfort	7.5	8	8.5
Economy	4	5	6
Safety	3.8	4.5	5
Brand equity	4	7	6
Service facilities	9	6	5

The figures are based on a scale from 0—10

On a different plane another matrix can be made with benefits on one axis and decision making concepts for each car separately, before the final decision is taken as follows:

Decision concepts/Benefits	Comfort	Economy	Safety	Brand equity
Beliefs				
Attitudes				
Perceptions				
Preferences				

There calls for a three-dimension matrix, which would help the decision makers. This is done in steps as given below:

1. Which attributes are used to define the product? (For example, for a car it could be its brand name, comfort or economy. For a house it could be its location, its construction and area.)
2. What is the possession level of the attributes in the product? (Is the car running very economical as compared to another car in the same category) This is really the value of the attribute, its perception in the customer's mind. Another example could be of an airline, where the passenger safety is of prime concern. However, the airlines never talk about the safety aspect as all airlines are supposed to be safe. They prefer to talk about, a/ ease of getting their tickets b/food c/ in-flight service and entertainment d. easy check-ins. And the customers form attitudes on the basis of these attributes.
3. What is the relative importance of each attribute in the overall product performance? In airline business is in-flight service more important than easy of getting tickets?
4. Do the customers weigh each of the attributes to reinforce their perceptions of overall product performance? How much weightage is given to each of the attributes and does it differ from customer to customer, or is product specific?

Note: At this stage the students should do an Attributes—Perception study for different products to find out how the customer's perceptions and preferences are formed.

It will be found that different customers have separate yardsticks for looking at the attributes. They trade off one against the other while making the purchase decisions as can be seen from the following example:

Some people buy car only for its brand name, e.g. Mercedes

Some buy car for its speed and power.

Yet others buy the car for its mileage only.

Some look for several of the attributes in some descending order of their importance. This is called the **Dictionary Rule.**

Dictionary Rule: If a customer finds two products having the first or the most important attribute to be equally present in both the products, and then they look for disparity in the next level attribute. They keep doing so till they arrive at the attribute where there is a difference in the two products. (In dictionary when you look for a word you go with its first alphabet and then to the next, so on, till you find the exact word.)

Buying a car, would the customer prefer lower price or better mileage? Can the seller charge one hundred thousand rupees more if the car gives 8km per litre more?

Multi-Attribute Analysis helps sellers to understand customers, who represent identifiable segments in terms of their perceptions and preferences.

Let us consider the levels of competition, or competitor's hierarchy. A competitor can be defined as the seller who compete for the same customer rupee as the widest competition level.

Narrowing it down, the competitors are those who sell same products from the same industry.

Further narrow definition of competitors would be the market segment competitors

To clarify the above let us take the Banking business.

First level would be the banking system, which would include Banks, Financial institutions, Non-banking financial institutions, merchant bankers and moneylenders.

Second level would be a bank who cater to the customers with a few of the banking products.

Third level is the bank in the same town or the same street.

Competition is becoming diversified as can be seen from the following:

1. Banking services have competition from software companies now, as a lot of on line Internet banking is being done with the help of relevant software.
2. Used cars compete with the new cars.

It is therefore possible to define competition by analyzing customer's data. It can be tried as given below:

- Define a product.
- Let the prospective customers decide the possible uses and benefits, as many as they can imagine the product is possessing. Can they think of other ways of getting the same benefits? This way the firms can get **Differential Competitive Analysis from the Customer's Viewpoint.**
- The customers should determine the products, which satisfy with their usage, and the benefits, which accrue to the customers from their use.
- The data thus obtained can be listed with priority as given by the customers.

The data thus obtained will provide the firm the information on the **Competitors for Each Product in Their Range.**

Summarizing it can be said that,

"Competitors analysis requires the prudent use of secondary and primary information to determine current and likely strategies. Customers can be employed to classify uses and benefits of products and to rank the competitors".

Let us see the **Assets and Skills** grid for competitors. These can be divided into two parts as follows:

1. **Primary:** Product development, product quality, product manufacturing cost, product differentiation, customer satisfaction and market share.
2. **Secondary:** Flexi-production, financial muscle, sales force, distribution network, brand image/equity, advertising and promotion, quality of service and growth of the market for the product.

Student's Discussion Points

1. Explain the principle of multi-attribute analysis.
2. Broad and narrow definition of competition.
3. How can a customer help in competitor's analysis?
4. Define unmet needs of the customers with examples.

Market Analysis

The following needs to be understood while analyzing the market:

- Market size, actual and potential
- Market growth prospects
- Market, product-wise profitability
- Cost structure
- Distribution pattern
- Success parameters

Market size and its growth can be assessed by knowing the demographic changes taking place in the market, income and salary growth of people in the market and changes in government policies relating to business of the products.

In the maturity and decline stage of PLC, the firm has to identify the following points:

- Price wars start if there is no product differentiation and there is over-capacity in production.
- Level of buyer's sophistication.
- Availability of substitution products.
- Why no growth, is there a new competitive product in the market?

To analyze the profit picture of a market the following points need to be seen:

- The types of competition in the market, is it a monopoly situation, oligopoly or fragmented market with a vast number of sellers. Market share of competitors and how are they safeguarding it, is it through price-cutting or brand management.
- How many new players are likely to join the competition? How serious are they and their potential threat as a competitor.
- How strong are the substitute products which vie for the customer's money?
- Bargaining power of suppliers.
- Bargaining power of buyers.
- For competitors the firm should know their number, size, and similarity of product, level of fixed costs and their exit barriers. For new entrants the firm should know the requirement of capital, economies of scale of the production, availability of distribution channels, raw materials and product differentiations.

High growth markets can suffer from overcrowding of players, penetrating prices, and technology changes and resources crunch.

Environment analysis makes the firm to understand the effect of changes in technology, macroeconomics, government policies, culture, demography and global.

Segmentation and Positioning

Segmentation allows the firms to focus on specified market sets through positioning, to enable the firm to launch a unique market program to stand out among competitors. Segmentation is essential as the customers have diverse needs and behaviour related to market stimuli. It also helps the firms as follows:

- Planning focused marketing programs.
- New product launches.
- Creating competitive advantage.

How to segment the customers? Following are the ways of market segmentation:

1. Benefit—to the customers, like better service needs, convenient pricing.
2. Product usage by the customers—like heavy usage, light usage.
3. Brand loyalty.
4. Product becomes a status symbol like Mercedes car.
5. Geographic—like the north, south, east and west of the country.

6. Demographic—based on age, income, place of residence, sex, religion.
7. Life style, psychographics divide.

Customer is known a king. Let us examine the statement. A guest stays in a hotel once in a year and another one stays six times in a year. It is the usage, which makes the customer the king or the commoner. The following matrix explains the point clearly with the help of customer of a five star hotel:

Yearly expense in rupees	10,000	25000	100,000	500,000	1000,000
Tourists in %	55	20	15	9	1
Business traveller in %	1	9	55	20	15

It is easy to describe the business traveller spending rupees 500,000 and above in a year as the king. (Of course, the hotels cannot ignore the small customers for; it is possible that today's common man may be the future king. Facilities like room upgrades, free use of gym are meant to have the king keep coming to the hotel.)

Social class too defines a business market segment, as people belonging to the same class tend to spend their money in buying the same things.

Business-to-Business or Industrial Segmentation

Industries buy raw materials and components from suppliers. The suppliers segment their customers as follows:

- **Company Size:** The larger the company the more product it is likely to buy, be better paymaster (as it has to keep its name as a good company). Sometimes medium size companies prove to be good as they are trying to grow and their reputation is vital for them.
- **Innovative Companies:** They have the lead user concept, want to be the first users of the product. Small companies have the advantage of being flexible in their production and other plans.

The following points make a good market segment:

1. The segment should be of adequate size. There should be manageable number of segments.
2. The segments should be concrete with justified measurable base for each segment.

While practically implementing the segment schemes, it is necessary to combine the descriptive variables like age, income for which data is available, with behaviour and attitude variables.

At times, sufficient data is not available for making a proper market segment, which is feasible too. There are product specific variables like, light users and heavy users and then there are general descriptive variables like demographic, geographic variables.

The focus should not however shift on just creation of a segment and segmentation should remain a tool of gaining Competitive Advantage.

Summarizing it can be said that,

"Markets are segmented to satisfy different customer needs to leverage as firm's advantage in size, location to serve identifiable groups of customers, profitably. From segmentation, the firm can target the segment or segments by steering its marketing efforts towards them."

Product Positioning involves focusing on a marketing program that one-segment customers will perceive as desirable and which will give the firm a differential advantage over competition.

Usually, there are a number of competitors for the same segment. Positioning gives the firm Sustainable Competitive Advantage because of its customer specific approach. The steps needed are

1. To identify relevant competition.
2. To draw the differential benefits and attributes significant to the segment where the firm scores better than competition.
3. Delineate firms and competitors current position.
4. Set out segments preferred attribute combinations.
5. Select positioning strategy.
6. Communicate the position.

Student's Discussion Points

1. Steps the Positioning Process.
2. Importance of communicating the difference between the firms and competitors product benefits and attributes. Does the firm have a position if the customer does not know about it?

In a nutshell, it can be said that

- Segmentation allows firms identify potential profitable group of customers.
- Positioning requires firms to identify the right competitors and differentiate their products and other Ps and then effectively communicate the unique benefits of these products to target customers.

Managing Across the Product Life Cycle (PLC)

With a lot of effort going into New Product development, firms have the benefit of introducing new products at some point of time. It is important that care is taken in managing the new introduction to ensure profits and volume business. Later on during the growth, maturity and decline stages of product life cycle proper management is required. The following figure gives the Product Life Cycle's different stages.

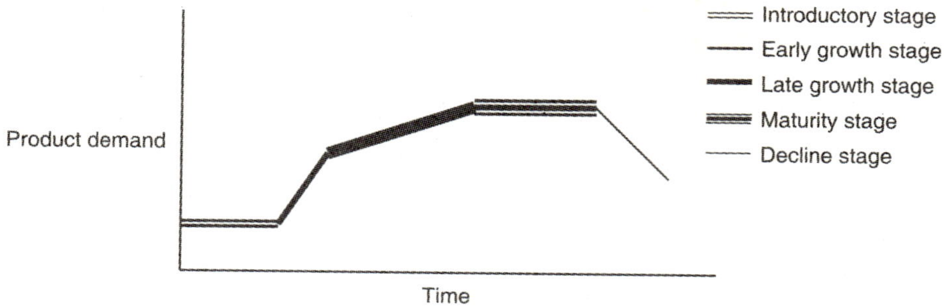

Strategies for Introductory Stage in PLC

Introductory stage is gaining importance by the day as, due to faster rate of obsolescence in most products the PLC is shrinking. New technologies are emerging in several products to make earlier product obsolete. Firms need to capture maximum market in this stage and as mostly there is little competition, they can charge skimming prices to get the maximum revenue. Main conditions in the introductory stage are as follows:

1. Growth is slow as the customers are not aware of the product and its concept. A lot of concept selling is required before actual volume business starts.
   (a) Product itself is not well defined.
   (b) Channels of distribution are also new, but since they have the customers coming to them for other products, they hold the key to business and have the power over the manufacturers.
   (c) Price—the rule of the game have not yet been finalized.
   (d) Advertising gives most of the information to competitors about the products, price, channels of distribution and its market segment, a thought out by the firm.
2. Only first introduction Firms have some advantage and other leaders and followers are not significant at this stage.
3. Penetrating prices are charged for gaining and maintaining the market share. With low prices, the firms spend good money on advertising and promotion. They depend on volume business and economies of scale in manufacturing for profits.
4. Skimming price is used when competition is yet far away. Customer base is narrow and the firms prefer not to spend a lot of money on advertising and promotion. Firms depend on high prices and low expenses for profits.
5. In case of skimming prices, competition comes in fast as they see the large margins of profits.

6. Penetrating prices keep competition away for quite sometime.

As can be seen the pioneering firms have the task of developing the market through concept selling, advertising and the later firms who follow get the benefit of their efforts. For example, suppose a firm introduces computers in a virgin underdeveloped market it will be doing concept selling telling advantages of using a computer to the customers. They will not be able to talk about their brand say, IBM. Later sellers like Compaq will be able to build on the concept acceptance of the customers and they can advertise their brands and generate brand awareness and brand loyalty, brand equity.

Summarizing, market pioneers managing the introductory stage of PLC, can pursue strategy to capture a narrow customer base with skimming prices for extra profits or they can plan on a broad market base with penetrating pricing.

Student's Discussion Points

1. What are the benefits and negative points of penetrating and skimming pricing policies?
2. What are some of the characteristics of the introductory stage of PLC?

In early growth stage market growth increases and the distinction between leaders and followers also grows. Product quality stabilizes and firm's dependency on channels reduces hence the power of channels also reduces, giving way to advertising and promotions besides personal selling by the firm's salespersons.

Hence it can be concluded that PLCs are identifiable and they require distinct marketing skills at each stage, especially at the introductory stage, when the failure risk and product costs are both high, quality often uneven and market acceptance is not fully assured.

Secondly, marketers have a choice of pricing the product in the introductory stage. They can either have widespread business with penetrating prices and market share, or to gain high unit profits with skimming prices.

Costs, Volumes and Experience Curve

Let us discuss how important are **Costs, Volumes and Experience Curve in our strategies for marketing. Marketing strategies are needed to balance core competencies of firms with business environment changes constantly taking place and are essential for the long term well being and growth of the firm. The basics of marketing are good strategies. Strategy needs an analysis of the firm, competition and customers in a dynamically changing business environment.**

Let us discuss the market leadership position a firm can enjoy. For getting volumes needed for leadership, the firm has to have penetrating prices. Hence, there is a cost of leadership, by way of reduced profit on unit product basis. In order to reduce the loss in profit the following is required to be done:

- Integrating marketing and production plans.
- Making an objective of High Volume and low cost production as a result.
- Focus on market share.
- Gain cost leadership.

Cost leadership is gained through the following methods:

1. Technological advancements.
2. Inputs from suppliers and customers for streamlining cost elements in manufacture.
3. Economies of scale, which help in reducing the Fixed Costs, as for larger production rentals, supervisor's salary and other overheads do not change and hence, unit fixed cost gets reduced.
4. Experience Curve which helps in reducing Variable Costs, as with passage of time, workers get to know the working better and wastage gets reduced, besides production time also shortens. With increase in cumulative workers experience in production, workers do better. This is most valid in

a. High labour cost industries

b. Complex assembly line operations

c. production of high numbers of standard products, which helps workers in repetitive work.

Experience curve cost reduction eomes from the following areas:

- Labour efficiency
- Work specialization and methods improvements
- New production process

It has been observed that experience improves performance from production equipment, changes in resource mix, material substitution. It helps in product standardization and redesign. **Experience effect results from the firm's attempt to achieve lower relative costs than the competition. Low cost production gives highest profit margins.**

Market Share Strategy

Firms are constantly striving to improve their market share. For this purpose the following strategies are planned:

- Plan large capacity production, which will help in achieving Economies of scale of production to reduce the fixed costs.

- Penetrating or aggressive pricing policy helps in getting larger market share as more customers, who are price conscious, buy the product. Initially, to gain a foothold in the market sellers resort to selling on marginal costs only where they put the price equal to the fixed cost plus a little element of variable cost. Once the market share is reached as planned, and brand loyalty gained from some customers, the price is increased to include both fixed and variable cost and some profit margin is also added to it. This is especially true for price sensitive segments of the market. The idea is to lower the price and in a way invest in future growth of the market. It can rebound if the market does not grow at all.

Let us discuss some successful cases of experience curve effect below:

- Manufacture of semiconductor devices, including ICs, initially the rejection rate used to be high, up to 50%. As the firms got experience in manufacturing, the workers could reduce the rejections and today the rejections are less than 1%. It has resulted in price reductions of not only these components, but also of the final electronic equipments.
- Honda motorcycles reduced prices substantially (in seven years, reduction in price was 100 US dollar due to experience effect).

The risks involved with gaining cost reduction through experience curve are given below:

- Manufacturers base their production plan as per the market forecasts. In case the demand projections prove to be wrong and demand fails to come to the anticipated levels, the cost reductions become void as then the production is tailored to the real demand only.
- Customer's tastes keep changing, more especially in fashion garments where the rate of obsolescence is high.
- Induction of new technology in manufacturing also reduces the effect of experience curve.
- Ego or other fixation on the old manufacturing process. The firms can argue that they had spent a lot of money in the old technology and they cannot abandon it so soon. Such mindsets are harming the growth of the firm as also reducing the benefits of experience as with the new technology the firm could achieve even better cost of manufacture.

Task for the Students

1. What are the factors responsible for reduction in costs once the sales volumes increase ?
2. Can the managers price products in anticipation of increases in volume sales ?

Summarizing, it can be said that

- Cost leadership is a powerful strategic tool where learning curve and economies of scale provide higher profits and better market share than that of the competitors.
- Economies of scale and learning curve effects must fulfil market needs. The firm must have the resources to finance the more effective operations.

Product Life Cycle—Growth Stage Strategy

Marketing strategies are needed at every stage of the life cycle to combat the market realities and the options available, as the firm and competitors relationships keep changing with the customers all the time.

Strategies for Early Growth Stage in PLC

Early growth involves large increases in volumes, and an increasing number of competitors as market players use advertising to build brand equity to elevate their market share and position. The following changes take place:

1. Sales volumes increase rapidly.
2. Competition rises.
3. Product design and specifications get standardized.
4. Firms plan their advertising and sales efforts to gain brand superiority.
5. Prices may start their downward slide.
6. Distribution network gets in to place and power over customers begins to move towards manufacturers from the channel members.
7. Demand shifts from primary one, say for a PC or CAR to secondary demand as, for Wipro PC or Honda City car, as people / customers become brand conscious.
8. At times the Pioneer, who started the sale of the product and did the initial concept selling, loses his superiority in growth stage to other players. **(Philips pioneered the audio cassettes, did the concept selling in competition with records, LPs EPs and 8 Tracks- they gave their technology to Sony who did well, better than Philips, during the growth stage)**

Growth stage means increase in demand and the manufacturers have to meet the demand. Their strategic options depend on the position they enjoy in the market as can be seen from below:

Let us take the firm's position as that of the **Market Leader** or that of **Market Follower**.

POSITION AS MARKET LEADER

Options—

- Fight————Maintain ————or Enhance
- Flight ————Exit ————or Fortify

For maintaining the market share the firm should increase its business as per the market growth and invest in advertising and selling on that basis.

For enhancing the market share firm should increase its market share at a faster or bigger than the market growth.

In real life situation if the firm plans only to maintain it may end up losing its market share and if it plans to enhance it may just be able to maintain its market share as competitors are also in with their plans.

The next option for some firms could be that of flight, giving up their leadership position. They can either exit or fortify i.e. get in to some niche market. At times the expenditure in maintaining the leadership position through is high and it eats away all the profits. Firms do plan to leave the leadership on such occasions.

HP Calculators gave their leadership to Texas Instruments and went in to niche market. HP had started in narrow market with low level of advertising efforts and they could raise the prices after leaving the market leadership.

POSITION AS A FOLLOWER

Let us examine the options followers have in the market. They can either take up the leadership position or remain as a follower. For each the choices can be as given below:

- Assume leadership————by copying the leader——or by leapfrogging by using latest techniques

In case of copying, the follower can do one better by learning from the mistakes committed by the leader? The follower thus challenges the leader. Follower also tracks the mistakes of the leader and turns them into opportunities.

If the leader is not making a mistake then the follower has to overtake the leader by using new technology, new plans and policies and he can leapfrog into leadership position.

A good example of leapfrogging is the leadership position now being enjoyed by the Japanese firms in the area of cars, which were the virtual monopoly of the Americans. In the area Consumer electronics also, Japanese firms have leapfrogged to leadership position. Japanese have taken recourse to improvements in process technology and not just planned better products. Re-engineering in production technology and innovative

distribution has helped them to do the leapfrogging. Hence, Japanese firms have gone for high volumes and economies of scale of manufacture. The customers do not see the new process; they see only better and economically priced products.

- The next option for the follower is to settle for being number two. There is only one number one possible and the second place helps in remaining focused (one firm advertises that we try harder to please the customer because we are number two.) they can cater to the customers who are not with the leader. The leader could be in the mass market spending large sums of money in advertising and promotion to stay number one. The second number could get in to a niche market. Or, follower could target all customers except those with number one, like the customer with the followers number three four etc. If the follower wants the third position then he can target the customers from the followers numbering four, five etc.

Strategies for Late Growth Stage in PLC

Late growth stage in the life cycle is where segmentation is a useful strategy to satisfy knowledgeable customers. Strategically, the firms need to either defend their position or find out unexplored niche markets.

The salient features of late growth stage are as follows:

- Sales volumes grows slowly
- Many competitors
- Price competition starts
- Excess capacity is likely to occur
- Channel members play one against the other to gain extra advantage.

Computer industry has suffered the world over as the growth in the last ten years reduced from a healthy 50% to only 25%. This has resulted in excess capacity and are resorting to promotional plans, they bundle a lot of software with the hardware as sales promotion. With lower demand and reduced production, the fixed costs per unit go up.

- Customers are very intelligent and demand a lot as specific benefits.
- Marketing efforts focus on specified segments.

In late growth stage customer's demands are more specific and market segmentation becomes critical. The strategies, which leaders and followers can pursue, are given below-

Leaders—target many segments

Followers—target a few segments only

Each segment needs a different type of at least one of the 4 ps.

With the excess production capacity and price pressures, the firms could decide to exit from the business altogether. The firm could need money for some other business and it plans to exit. Sometimes the follower has leapfrogged to leadership and the leader may decide to exit.

Summarizing it can be concluded as follows:

1. Early and late growth stages of the product life cycle, are having different increases in sales volumes which require different strategic initiatives.
2. Leaders and followers have separate strategic requirements in all stages of life cycle.

Task for the Students

1. What is the difference between early and late growth stage?
2. What are the factors, which could be responsible for a firm leaving the market even in growth stage?

Strategies for the Maturity Stage in PLC

When the products reach the maturity stage, their demand growth stops, it reaches a plateau. Firms need to manage the sales in this stage either for cash or they should plan product differentiation or geographic extension of the markets, in the country or through exports. However, if opportunity costs exceed present value benefits, it is better to exit from the product sales.

Mature markets are known for sophisticated buyers, well-organized segments, reduced differences in products from competition and stable sales volumes.

Maturity stage has the following main characteristics–

1. Constant sales volumes year to year.

2. Product differentiation vanishes as competition also makes "ME TOO" products.

It is however, not necessary that in a product range all the models may be in the same stage of life cycle e.g. in cars one model may have reached maturity and other may be in introductory stage.

Sustainable Competitive Advantage (SCA) – SCA can be achieved by differentiating one or more of the following, in maturity stage–

- Service
- Distribution
- Advertising of intangible benefits like brand equity, service
- Product differentiation does not make much of an impact in maturity stage

- Pricing takes a toll and it has to be competitive—in India, with new models coming Maruti had to reduce its price.
- Buyers are knowledgeable, know about firms and competitive products are discerning and have bargaining power.
- There are relatively few new buyers. Firms, when they want to increase sales, either take customers from the competition or they fight for the small number of new buyers. In most cases some old buyers quit the field and the new ones replace them.

Let it be understood that for most products, except for FMCGs taking customers from competition is a difficult task as any action, like price reduction can lead to price war and the lower price can in any case be met by competition leaving the market share on status-quo.

In maturity stage, leaders and followers have different strategic options available to them. Leaders may mature products as cash cows or they may harvest for profits. Followers may try tom keep the market share at the existing level, grow or even exit as per the following plan:

Leaders—a. manage for cash——————or, b. harvest, i.e. reduce market share by going for niche market.

Followers—maintain the market share————grow————exit

Maintaining or increasing market share needs investments and therefore reduces profits. Market share ceases to be of any importance in maturity stage. Followers can take the leadership position if the leaders are quitting it or taking followers position. However, the followers must find out the reasons why the leaders are leaving the top spot; is there a new technology available now? Market segmentation is the key to success in this stage. It is necessary to offer specific benefits to a group of customers or to the segment. It is of importance if the switching costs of customers for changing products are low.

Task for the Students

1. What are the strategic implications in maturity stage with highly sophisticated buyers?

2. How can firms keep gross margins high in the maturity stage?

Let us see how the firm's can keep prices high in the maturity stage. They can have distinct product differentiation to keep the switching costs high. They can build their brand equity high and have superior service. These intangible benefits will place the product in the customers mind set; keep competition away and the firms can still manage high profit margins.

Summarizing, the mature markets are stable with few major players and reduced product differences among competitors. These markets also provide cash for invigorating newer product concepts.

Ford car was down in dumps in 1980. Then the new President Don Peterson told his management team ,"Get the best features of the cars worldwide, without omitting any feature, including door handles and glove compartments size," Ford was back on its feet in less time than was envisaged.

Strategies for the Decline Stage in PLC

Decline stage in life cycle is characterized by decrease in Sales Volume as a result of product demand, demographic changes, and technological changes over a period of time. Cheaper substitute products and changes in customer's tastes also account for the decline stage.

Key factors which are present in the decline stage are given below:

- Over capacity in production
- Severe price competition
- Several competitors exit.

For at least getting the fixed cost, sales are made with low profit margins, as it is not easy to reduce production. However, if fixed costs are low then the firm can plan to downsize the production. If variable costs are high, exiting is easy otherwise on high variable cost it is not so. Success in maturity stage through fixed costs help the firms survive in decline stage as well. With high fixed costs it is easy to get in to penetrating prices.

The marketing strategies for **Decline Stage** are as given below:

	Hospitable market	Inhospitable market
Leaders	Maintain lead	Harvest
Followers	Harvest	Divest

Hospitable market in decline stage, is when the rate of decline is slow, otherwise it becomes inhospitable. For leaders in hospitable market, they can keep their market going down at the rate the market is declining. For harvesting the firms bring down their market share and try to get in to a niche market. In inhospitable market the follower's best strategy is to exit from the market. Marketing mix wars begin in decline stage starting from price war. It should however be understood that the players are all fighting over a shrinking pie. Penetrating prices, higher investments in advertising and promotion mark the decline stage. It becomes a vicious circle like the arms race of the twentieth century between the USA and erstwhile USSR and hence should be avoided by the firms. Several firms decide to get out of the market. However, the firm which decides to stay, gets in to monopoly situation and can reap the skimming price benefits till the market remains.

One firm in India was making Radio Valves and as most radio manufacturers changed to using semiconductor devices, other valve manufacturers in the world stopped making them resulting in monopoly for the firm. As there was some market in Africa the firm could charge better than Indian market price, skimming price for a few years before the demand dwindled to zero.

In case of some product being reintroduced in the market, the last survivor gets the benefit.

Summarizing, "A life cycle audit helps the firms in determining where their products are placed in the life cycle so that their marketing can be strategically planned.

Hence the firms need to do a **Life Cycle Audit** as follows:

Competitive position leaders/ followers	Introductory stage	Growth stage	Maturity stage	Decline stage
Objectives				
Target customers				
Product				
Price				
Distribution				
Advertising				
Promotion				

The audit summarizes the entire life cycle. It is possible to plan strategies for the entire life cycle with built-in contingency.

Portfolio Management Analysis

Portfolio analysis takes into account that large multi-product firms have synergies within and they need to provide recourses for growing their attractive businesses, divesting poor performers with unattractive profits/or losses. They need to divert resources from mature and stable businesses into attractive promising businesses.

Portfolio analysis empowers managers to balance future and current opportunities by assessing business attractiveness and competitive position in a two dimensional matrix.

Firms have a life of their own, as a single product firm will dies if that product fails. Managers want multi-product firm to ensure that some product would be in growth stage always. Portfolio analysis is managed as follows-

- Focus on two major dimensions of marketing strategy.

- Look for business attractiveness to assess how good is the business opportunity and relative competitive position to understand if the firm can be a winner.
- Understanding of different resource needs – some business need resources and others have excess resources.

Resources can be defined as finance, human, technology, information and managerial.

So far the discussion has been on getting the competitive advantage for individual product. However, in case of a multi-product firm, emphasis should be on managing the products together and not separately. For making an analysis of firm's strength the **Boston Consultancy Group, BCG**, have developed a matrix as given below:

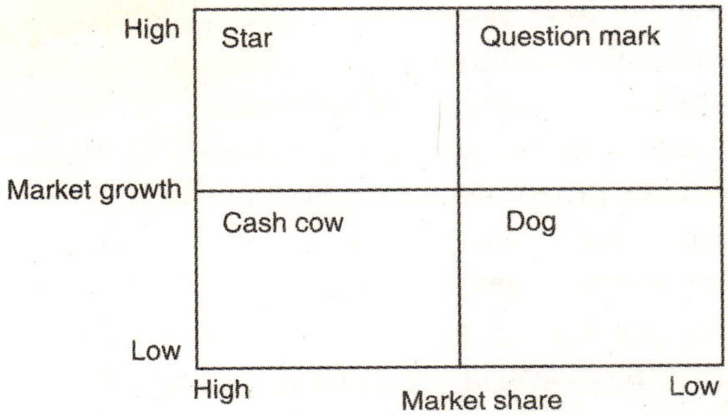

In BCG Matrix, the horizontal axis shows the market share of the product and the vertical axis shows the market growth.

Let us see the position of products in different quadrants-

Quadrant Star - in this quadrant the market growth of the product is high and the firm's product enjoys high market share. It is characterized by the following:

- The firm's product enjoys a strong market position that of the leader.
- The market growth of the product is high and attractive.
- Competitor's better technology and superior market acceptance can make the firm's business risky, even if enjoys leadership position.
- Low profits, as the leader has to spend large amount on marketing advertising to maintain the leadership.
- High expenditure required for marketing mix factors.

Strategic options in Star Quadrant are as follows:

1. **Increase share:** Invest in anticipation of higher market growth. Put entry barriers for newcomers through pricing, innovative distribution and advertising.

2. **Maintain share:** Have good market intelligence to be able to counter their actions. Invest in marketing mix selectively

Quadrant Question Mark - In this quadrant, the market share is low although the growth of the market is high. The position of the product is as follows-

- The product is in growth stage while the firm's product is having low market share.
- The firm has the opportunity to increase its market share by investing in advertising and promotion.
- It is often a new entrant. It could be that all players are new or one could have assumed leadership in the market.
- Risks are high, technology and basic product acceptance in the market is not fully established.
- Negative profits and huge expenses in marketing for either concept selling or for increasing market share.
- Needs long-term and strong commitment of the management for the product's growth to attain Star position.
- The firm must decide to how many of its products are in this quadrant and how many of them can it support on long-range basis.
- The firm could get in to some niche market segment.
- If the firm has several products in this quadrant, and you keep all, you are in a strategic trap, because it cannot place proper resources for them and is in danger of losing all.

Quadrant - Cash Cow is where the firm has high market share but the market growth is low. The firm can reduce its marketing expenses as it is already in dominant marketing position and can become low cost supplier. The firm can have the following market situation-

- Dominant market position
- Slow market growth
- Low cost supplier
- Good profit and cash generation
- Low market risk

Strategies for Cash Cow Quadrant are as given below:

1. Manage for cash, maintain market share
2. Requires cautious investment in market as growth is low
3. Cash generation can be used for products in question mark quadrant
4. Harvest- go for niche market if future prospects are low
5. Divest if product demand is going down at a rapid pace, because of new technology products have come into the market, or because the customer's tastes have been changing.

Quadrant Dog: In this quadrant, the market growth is weak and the firm has low market share. The market situation can be described as given below-

- Weak market position
- Slow market growth
- High cost supplier
- Poor or no profit and cash generation. However, by managing it carefully, using the niche market route it can be profitable too
- Several times the product could be basee on management ego as once it was a star product
- High management turnover, as the product is not doing well, "customers know us because of this product."
- The product takes a lot of management time in planning its strategies for hardly any gain.

Strategies for Dog Quadrant are given below:

1. Maintain market share for whatever cash the product generates
2. Plan for changing or adding some market segments.
3. Stop all new investment in the product
4. Divest – sell and use the funds for other products in question mark stage
5. Keep the product for any goodwill it may have or there are strong exit barriers.
6. Turn around – by innovating, product differentiation, downsizing
7. Get into niche market

Investment Cycle for the BCG Matrix, therefore is as given below:

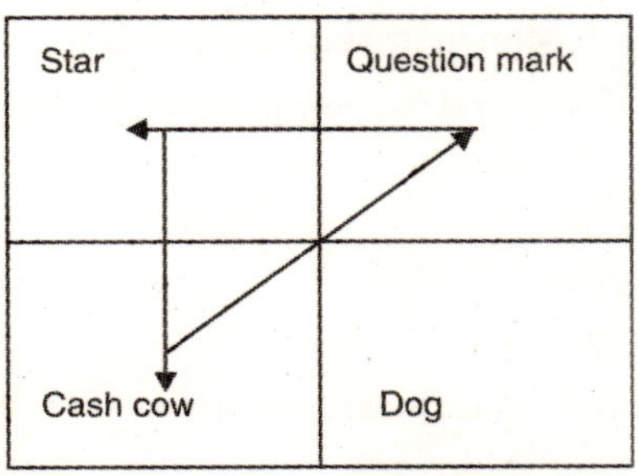

The extra cash generated in cash cow stage is invested in the question mark stage to bring the product in to star stage. Over time the market growth of star product goes down when it reaches the maturity stage of its life cycle, and it starts having extra cash, which is invested in question mark stage to complete the cycle.

The BCG Matrix has been fine tuned by the GE Model, which can be used to define markets and products position as follows:

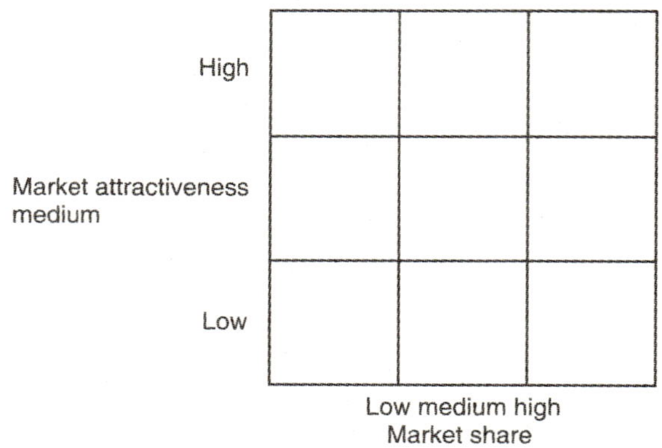

In the GE Matrix the market attractiveness and firm's market share for a product can be platted as high, medium and low, thus enabling the firm to understand the position more accurately and plan its strategies accordingly.

Market attractiveness can be measured as given below:

- Market size and growth
- Degree of market concentration, is it localized or is it spread out
- Industry profitability
- Price sensitivity of demand
- Exit and entry barriers
- Strength of channel members
- Rate of obsolescence or technology change

Firm's market share and its competitive position can be seen from the following:

- Market share
- Profit margins
- Brand loyalty
- Degree of product differentiation
- Proprietary technology
- Financial position
- Personnel

Summarizing, market share and market potential are mapped in a portfolio analysis to provide a visual understanding of the industry players and the attractiveness and competitive positions of the firm's products.

Portfolio analysis can be used to find out where resources should be deployed and to determine the relationship among and competitors.

Task for the Students

1. Discuss the strengths and weaknesses of portfolio analysis.

Case Study

Activity Base Corporation—ABC is a multi-product firm with all India sales networks. While the firm has been growing at the market rate of growth, its profit picture has been rather dismal. The management has appointed a firm of consultants to recommend them the action they should be taking to improve their bottom line. Some details of the firm are given below for student's perusal-

- Annual sales Rs. 145 crores
- Raw Material cost Rs. 50 crores
- Fixed costs Rs. 15 crores
- Available revenue Rs. 80 crores
- Product costs Rs. 65.5 crores
- Profit before tax Rs. 14.5 crores
- Total Rs. 80 crores

The next table gives the product-wise picture of revenue generation, share of cost, net revenue value, cost to profit coefficient.

S.No.	Rev. value	Rev % of total	Cost value	Cost % of total	Net revenue value	% of net revenue value	Cost-profit coeff.	Remarks
1.	19	24	18.2	28	0.8	5	0.25	
2.	14	17.5	16.7	25.5	– 2.7	–12	Loss	
3.	14	17.5	7.2	11	6.7	4.7	3.3	
4.	11	14	5.2	7.5	5.8	40	3.8	
5.	7	9	5.4	8	10.6	11	1.5	
6.	4	5	3.4	5	0.6	4	1.0	
7.	4	5	3.6	5	0.4	3	0.75	
8.	3.5	4.5	3.3	5	0.2	1.5	0.5	
9.	2	2.5	1.85	2.5	0.15	1	0.5	
10.	1	1	1.5	2	– 0.5	– 0.5	Loss	

The next table gives the management support as it exists for each product. Students can use the table to diagnose the problem I, of each product and plan strategies accordingly.

S. No.	Revenue	Working capital	Management support	Technical support	Sales service support	Remarks
1.	19	15	Very high	Very good	Very good	
2.	14	4.5	Very high	Very good	Very good	
3.	14	5	Very high	Low	Medium	
4.	11	3	High	Low	Medium	
5.	12	0.5	Nil	Low	High demand	
6.	4	Nil	High	High	Best	
7.	4	Nil	High	High	Best	
8.	3.5	15	Spl. task force	Very good	High pressure	
9.	2	5	Low	Low	Low in sale high for old products	
10.	1	Nil	High	High	Nil	

Task for the Students

Formulate strategies for each product taking its position in the BCG Matrix considering revenue generation and support given and needed. Working capital needs give you a clue to the monitory support provided to each product. Can you find out which products are in the star, cash cow, question mark and dog stages of the BCG Matrix?

The study of strategic marketing should make the student aware of the necessity of the study as in today's market business environment keeps changing rapidly and unless fast decisions are taken the firms are going to be left behind in the competitive race. It helps the firm to make long range plans to remain proactive and avoid fire fighting measures which firms keep taking today. It also helps in taking short-term actions to beat the competition in instable conditions.

Firms are able to make the right investment decisions and also plan resource allocations in the areas, which bring the desired results and avoid supporting loss-making investments. Communications through the organization and inter-organization to the suppliers and buyers can be directed to help the firm in achieving its objectives. Most importantly, it helps firms in dealing with changes taking place in the business environment most effectively to its full advantage.

Time is the essence of success in business. What needs to be done must be done with a sense of urgency and therefore, it is imperative for the firm to keep a continuous scan of the environment factors, both general and competitive, and take proactive decisions for continued success. Otherwise, the firms will remain in the fire-fighting mode all the time trying to cope up with the immediate and current problems and will not be able to take advantage of the opportunities the business environment keeps generating all the time.

❍❍❍

3

SALES MANAGEMENT PROCESS—CONCEPT OF PERSONAL SELLING

3.1 INTRODUCTION

In the context of exchange of goods for cash two terms are used, marketing and sales. Marketing is the overall umbrella, which covers product itself, product marketing research, pricing, distribution, promotion and sales. A sale considered complete when the actual transaction takes place and money is exchanged for goods. Hence sales assume a great deal of importance in the game of marketing.

Many firms, considering the importance of both marketing and selling have separate Marketing Manager and Sales Manager for the two functions.

Sales Managers have the following roles to perform in the firm:

1. Defining sales policy of the firm
2. Marketing research
3. Pricing and terms of business
4. Distribution
5. Advertising, publicity and promotion
6. Selection, training and motivation of the salesmen
7. Sales territory allocation
8. Sales target for each territory
9. Sales forecasting
10. Expense budget for the department and for each salesman
11. Selling cost control
12. Reporting and control system.

The Sales Policy of a firm starts with selection of product(s) for sale, pricing of products, geographic coverage, distribution arrangements, distribution logistics, advertising, promotion and publicity plans. The policy is decided after the final approval of firms CEO, who considers the financial aspects of the policy before approving it.

Since marketing research, pricing, distribution, advertising and promotion have been covered in the book chapters; these are not being repeated here.

Selection, Training and Motivation of Salesmen—In the early part of the twentieth century, Salesmen were considered as gifted individuals, born with persuasive skills. Later on it has been proved that if the right type of candidate is selected he can be trained to become a Top class salesman. Firms therefore look for the right kind of recruit for the job who can be trained in the firm's culture and way of working. Getting the right people is difficult task as the breed of good salesman material is a rare commodity. Firm's Human Resource Managers, therefore use all possible methods to locate the right people.

Selection of Salesmen/Saleswomen—The usual method of selection is through the candidates' bio-data and interview. The Sales Manager is guided by the following factors while selecting his sales team:

1. Product to be sold, its technology, usage
2. Size of the firm
3. Distribution channels
4. Level of the customers to be met, e.g., Purchase Assistants, Technical Managers, or Managing Directors
5. Selling aptitude
6. Knowledge of the trade
7. Knowledge of the market, channels
8. Knowledge of local language
9. Knowledge of a foreign language, if the salesman has to be posted out of the country.
10. Product knowledge
11. Health, as travelling takes a big toll on the salesmen's health.
12. Duties of salesmen, Showroom or field work.

Aptitude for selling obviously is important, which includes, ability to make friends easily, hard work, plenty of travelling, negotiating skills and a genuine desire to help others, especially the customers, within the ambit of work or even outside of it. The salesmen can acquire most of the other characteristics but the aptitude must be within the person.

It is unfortunate that for actual selection of sales persons, only the age old methods are still in vogue, The Human Resource person sees the applications, which at times are in the shape of a questionnaire given by the firm and filled by the candidates. To assist the Sales Manager, the HRD people have the first interview of the candidates, which at times assumes the role of interrogation which cover varied aspects of the candidate's life from childhood onwards, social activities, leisure time activities. Several executives can take the interview. At times a written test is given, which is screened by psychologists, to find out the candidates reactions in times of stress. In some firms these are needed and in others may be only means of eliminating from selection some candidates, on the basis of personal bias.

Appointment of Sales Persons— Since the duties of salesmen are mostly in the field, without any direct supervision it is important that the terms of service in the organization are clearly set out, including, duties, responsibilities, and authorities.

The authorities given to the salesmen assume great importance as the salesmen bind the firm in contracts involving large amounts of moneys. Terms of business inclusive of prices, payment terms, and delivery periods can be effective sales tools, and yet used incorrectly they can bring huge losses to the firm besides damage to the firm's reputation. Quotations given by the salesmen in the field need to be within the given parameters, and the authority to change the terms, e.g. price should be well defined and given in writing to avoid bad blood later on. (For big, major deals the Sales Manager is usually handily available to the salesman for advice or even assists in closing the negotiations, if the salesman feels the need.)

Credit as a sales tool is well accepted in business and yet unless creditworthiness is fully assessed care needs to be taken. Firms should have a credit rating form, which includes details about the customer's ability and willingness to pay dues well in time. Cash rich firms should NOT be taken as good paymasters as ability and willingness are two different things as far as credit is concerned.

Guarantees—Offer of guarantee to the customer constitutes focus of quality by the seller. Guarantee cost money and extending the guarantee period can prove to be expensive to the seller. Most new salesmen are not aware of the hidden costs involved in offering extended guarantees. Salesmen tend to quote, almost always incorrectly, the competition as having given increased guarantee to some obscure customer, to get a little leverage from the management in their selling effort. Proper investigations by the Sales Manager would reveal the truth in such cases and final decision can be taken only after such investigations have been made. Offer of extended guarantee is usually taken by the Sales Manager for the entire business, unless it is some tender business, especially government tender, where spot decisions are needed to be taken. In such cases, the salesman should be given the authority to make the changes in guarantee offered, if required. Similarly, at times special concessions are offered to get bulk orders, which would need the same type of care on the part of the salesman and the Sales Manager.

One area in which most salesmen want authority is in settling of customers' claims. When the product sold is defective, stale, and un-saleable or not up to the sample shown or specifications given, then the customer is entitled to get compensation for the same. In such cases the salesman should be authorized to give credit towards the claim, to ensure that customer goodwill is maintained. However, if the claim is quite large then the salesman should involve the Sales Manager in the decision making process and should inform the customer of the importance, the firm gives to the customer, that the Sales Manager is looking in to the compensation against the claim. Such disputes are common when the customer is a channel member. The reputation of making genuine claims should be taken into account while settling claims of the channel members.

Some unscrupulous salesmen are known to obtain customers goodwill by allowing bigger credit than justified to make personal reputation rather than giving the right amount of credit. They even give a sob story of the firm's officers, who, they claim are not knowledgeable enough and that is why they have negated the salesman's recommendation regarding the claim. One wrong settlement of claim in favour of the customer could open floodgates, at times fuelled by competitors, that customers from other geographic areas could be making a bee line for getting their fake claims settled because of the bad precedence of one case.

3.2 ROLE OF SALES MANAGER

Sales Territory Allocation—It is the job of the sales manager to ensure that the salesmen in his department are usefully employed, given equitable workload and can produce the best results. For this purpose, sales managers have to distribute the entire geographic area of business in salesmen's territories, which become the sole responsibility of individual salesman with regard to the sales activities in the areas. As the product range differs widely so methods of territory allocation can be seen from the following:

- Consumer products—as the customer groups are wide spread geographically, the territories are divided as given below:

  (i) Equitable sales potential—(While dividing north India Rajasthan may have lower potential and hence it could be added to the Haryana state)

  (ii) Concentration of business (If Delhi state has large potential it could be considered as an independent territory)

  (iii) Ease of territory coverage, which will help in reducing the back tracking for the salesman

  (iv) Product range specific areas on the basis of demographic division—for product for low income groups territory could be the jhuggi-jhonpadi clusters, the slum areas in a town.

- Industrial products—as the customers are usually located in a cluster, several textile mills in one district–Ahemdabad, the territories are allocated on the bases of potential, of business in each cluster and the degree of difficulty in getting the business, competitors hold on the customer and the need for providing technical service to the customers.

Sales Targets—Based on the availability of product to the sales manager in one year, through the firm's own production or through outside procurements, the sales manager plans to sell the entire quantity of products. He fixes his own target for the year, which is then divided in to targets for each of the sales territories. The common method of target fixation is given below:

- Territory's total business potential
- Strength of the sales team
- Competitive strength
- Environment's effect on business in the territory
- Target should be reachable but with a stretch.

Given below is a format used for allocation of sales targets:

Sales Manager's Target **Period 2002-2003**

	Territory A	Territory B	Territory C	Territory D
PCs				
Modem				
Printers				
UPS				

The target is divided for each territory as follows:

Territory A

Sales executive	PCs	Modem	Printers	UPS
A				
B				
C				
D				

Each sales executive fixes the target of his dealers based on past performance, market potential, which is discussed with the dealer before finalization. One method of keeping record, dealer-wise as also monitoring dealer sales is given below, which shows product sales for each dealer on monthly basis and compares the sale with sales of the same month in the year/s gone by. This lets the salesman to locate the weak areas (products) in case of each dealer and helps the salesman in finding solutions for the decline in sales. This can be worked on progressive basis, which would indicate the salesman the dealer's performance on a cumulative pattern for the year.

The statistics can be generated with the help of computers by feeding the sales invoices in to it.

Dealers name

Products	Sale Jan. 2002	Sale Jan.-May 2002	Sale Jan. 2001	Sale Jan.-May 2001
PCs	547	2740	475	2500
Modem	34	150	42	173
Printer	65	351	45	254
UPS	120	450	140	520

As can be seen the dealer has done well in PCs and printers as compared to last year while they are worse off in modems and UPS. The salesman must find out the reasons for the ups and downs and ensure that the ups remain that way and the downs come up. In this manner, the salesman would be able to evaluate the stress needed for each product and each dealer. Other areas of interest would be the growth pattern of the market, competitive share holding, effect on sale of the firm and competition of respective advertising and sales promotion of the competing firms. The increase in market share comes from either totally new customer who has not bought before at all and from taking competitors, customers and each firm is trying for the same. The exception to the rule is when the firm decides to opt for only niche market leading to final divestment when the product is in decline stage of the PLC. The salesmen need to organize their work and time in a manner that desired results are ensured. For the purpose, they need to plan the work for which they need the following inputs:

- Territory map giving locations of the main distributors, dealers, retailers, direct customers. This helps in tour planning when the salesmen can avoid backtracking by planning going in loops to cover the entire territory without having to resort to going back and forth.

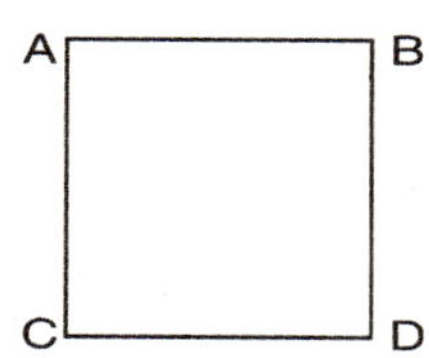

Starting from point A the salesman can go to B then to C and D. If he goes from A to D and then comes back to A before going to B then he is wasting time and travelling expense. Structured tours help the customers and many firms believe that if the customers, including the channel members know that the firm's salesman will visit on the tenth of each month then they prepare themselves for the meeting at the agenda can be gone through in quick time and the desired result achieved. It also gives the impression of professionalism of the firm to the customers.

In case of industrial products, the target fixation takes into account new customers (industries) emerging in the area, general and competitive environment and demand pattern of the final product of the customers. Business to Business sales requires the following extra ingredients for successfully meeting the targets.

The increase in Business Management schools have made their life a little easier as the schools provide skilled persons with basic grounding in management.

Firms look for the following qualities in their salesmen:

- An aptitude for hard work
- Technical knowledge as required for selling the product
- Positive outlook
- Good communication skills, both oral and written
- Extrovert personality
- Helpful nature
- Requisite experience, if it is not in a management trainee position

Human Resource Managers get the persons in one of the following ways:

- Promotions from inside the firm
- Competitors personnel
- Casual applications received by them
- Business schools campus interviews
- Advertisements in the press
- With the help of recruiting agencies.

For technical products the inside promotions can be useful as they know about the product and can start becoming productive in less time. However, the inside person should have the basic selling attitude. For example, if he is not keen on travelling he cannot succeed in a selling career. Competitors' staff knows the business and can become useful, provided they are not the one's being off-loaded by the competitor because of their inefficiency.

Good firms usually have a databank of applications received by them, which have been sent by people, unsolicited, as they are interested in taking up a job with the firm. Such applications must be screened to find out if they contain any suitable candidates who can be called for a personal interview.

For Sales Trainee positions, the business schools are a good source and most good firms are regularly going there for campus interviews.

Press advertisements are a bit expensive, but they get the best rewards as, people who meet the exact specific requirements only apply and from them the right person/s can be selected.

In most towns a number of recruiting agencies have come up. They are good sources of candidates as they do all the spadework like going through the bio-data sheets, short-listing the right candidates who can be interviewed by the firm for final selection. These have been doing a good job as far as recruitment of senior persons is concerned.

The first task of the Sales Manager is to clearly write down the exact requirements, as specifications, like, "We need sales trainees, either sex, between twenty and twenty five years of age. Science graduates with management education will be preferred. "A mention of the product/s they will sell and an idea of the remuneration they will get, is necessary to get the right candidates for interview.

Training of Salesmen—Here are three main methods of providing training to the new entrants in the sales organization of a firm:

1. Class room training where the trainee is told about the plans, policies, methods of working, hierarchy levels, reporting levels, forms used in report writing. Besides, they are given extensive product knowledge, they are told about products benefits for the customers, its USP, and its comparative value with respect to competitive products.
2. On the job training when they work as understudy of one senior experienced salesman, watch him how to negotiate the sales deals and generally plans his work on a day-to-day basis.
3. Training on the job is like learning how to swim once the person is thrown inside the pool. For people with initiative and drive this is the best method. It allows the trainee to learn at his own speed unencumbered with some senior who may have become cynical because of his length of service and perhaps no promotion.

Besides the training given at the start, salesmen should keep receiving Refresher Courses to ensure that they are updated on to the firms' plans, new products and changes in the business environment. Such courses can be planned in-house or at a Training Institute, which offers such programs for the corporate executives in different disciplines in management.

Motivating the Salesmen — Salesmen are high-strung individuals with wide vision, initiative, drive, resourcefulness who have the ability to go out to face the customers. The customers come in a variety of temperaments moods views and the salesmen have to fine-tune their own behaviour pattern according to the customers'. Salesmen believe in hard work, are result oriented and seldom broach interference in their work, not even from their superiors in the firm. They believe that they are the Stars of the firm and should be treated as such. However, like all individuals, salesmen too need appreciation of their work and that becomes the biggest motivating factor for them. A healthy rivalry amongst the salesmen of a firm is another motivating factor. Firms plan sales contests within the sales team, with awards for the best performers. To ensure that the contests are effective and bring the desired result, they should be planned on the following lines:

- Each salesman should be given a target to achieve clearly in writing.
- The contest should be on a time bound basis
- Weight-age should be given to the strength of the competitors in each salesman's area.
- If there are several products, targets should be each one of them and not just for the one's where the sale is lagging from previous periods.
- The basis of targets should be historical sales of products in each area, plus any major change, which may have taken place, like development of new industrial centres.
- Judgment of contest winners should be done without any bias to prove fair play by the management.
- Winners should be given awards, acclaimed in the firm's newsletter and if the performance keeps improving, then they can be promoted. (Promoting salesmen can be at times counter-productive because a good field man may not prove to be a good officer. In fact several salesmen in the USA even refuse desk, better paid jobs, because they do not want to miss the independence and the thrill of field work.)
- Complete knowledge of the customer's requirements, problems which need to be solved.
- Level of technology involved in marketing the product. This would decide if a technical salesman should be making the call.
- Product knowledge and the benefits it offers to the customer in terms of safety of operations, economy, ease of usage and storage.

The itinerary for both B to B and consumer product salesman should be made on the following format (specimen only subject to change as per individual firms needs):

Salesman ________________ Area________________ Month _________

Date	Place	Customer	Person(s) to be met	Purpose of the visit	Brief outcome/follow up needed in time frame

The full report of each visit should be on a format specimen given below:

1. Customer-, firm's name, address, phone, fax, email
2. Persons met with designation and vested authority
3. Files, documents, literature, testimonials taken and discussed with the customer.

4. Objectives of the visit. It is useful to have one major and a few minor objectives, which should be in line with the major objective. In case the major objective is not achieved in a particular visit the salesman can try to achieve that least one of the minor objectives. Major objective of sales call is usually to get the purchase order. Minor objective could be to invite the customer for a product demonstration.
5. A brief account of the discussion held and the customer's viewpoint on the benefit story given for the product.
6. Result of the visit. Follow up action required, giving the names of the people who would take the action along with the time schedule for the same.
7. In case of retailers/dealers the report format can be made as given below:

Dealer **Date**

Product	Stock with the dealer	Last months sale	Average monthly seasonal sale	Purchase order received/enclosed
PCs	12	7	12	25
Modem	7	8	5	10
Printers	8	5	8	10
UPS	4	8	10	25

As can be seen the dealer is running low on UPS stocks and the order execution should be carried out quickly to avoid loss of business. In some products extra stocks create a sales push on to the dealer, who has to reduce the inventory and blocked money and space and therefore he tries his best to sell the maximum quantities. A column can be made for giving the details of advance money received from the dealer towards the order.

Sales Forecasts and Budgeting

Different firms have separate defined periods for which they want a sales forecast. The forecasts or budgets help the firm in the following activities:

- Building production quantities
- Controlling inventory levels
- Planning distribution network changes, if required
- Pricing decisions
- Recruitment, training of salesmen
- Increase in geographic coverage of sales
- Providing technical support to the sales team.
- Providing after sales service, guaranty and warranty services.

Sales forecasts are made on the sales territory basis and then they are consolidated to get to the all India figure. In the first half of the twentieth century, sales forecast was made for periods ranging from one to seven years. It was possible to give long ranging forecast because the business and competitive environment were not changing much. In case of seven years forecast, it was assumed that the deviation level of each forward year could increase by five percent. In other words the first year the variation accepted between the actual sales seen after the year and the forecast could be within the range of plus, minus five percent. Next year it could go to ten per cent and in the seventh year the variation could be as high as thirty-five per cent.

Today, the forecasting is being done for one year, which is reviewed quarterly to dovetail the production to the best fit for the market being catered to. In case of large value products the production is undertaken on the basis of orders received only to avoid inventory pileups. The forecast chart looks as given below:

Territory **Salesman**

Products	2000	2001	2002	2003	2004	2005	2006
PCs	124	136	140	165	175	190	240
Modem	23	21	29	38	45	65	90
Printer	10	15	25	35	60	75	123
UPS	12	16	25	35	60	70	85
Laptops	7	12	15	25	45	70	95

Sales forecast for the entire country is the sum total of the forecasts of all the territories plus the plans for exports made by the sales manager. Forecasting export trade is done on the following basis:

- Country wise sales plans
- Service facilities needed in each country
- Competitive products
- General and competitive business environments of the countries
- Political stability of the country
- Relationship with the foreign government.

3.3 LOCATING NEW CUSTOMERS

Marketers have to keep locating new customers. This exercise can be termed as Prospecting. In prospecting the sales person has to identify and qualify new customers as this is one of the most important ways of creatively getting new business. The next step is to set up an objective for calls on the customers as well as on prospects. The sales person must know how to gather essential information about the prospect before making call plans. Next the call tactics need to be formulated.

The sales person needs to have the right attitude before the call and this attitude can be developed. The sales person should ensure that he gets the prospect interested in his preposition quickly enough. It is always useful to verify the efficacy of the call plans.

The sales person must be fully aware of the features of the product or the service he has to sell. He must be able to distinguish between the features and the derived benefits from the features of the product. This will help him in putting together an effective presentation while maintaining the prospect's interest and believability in the presentation. Most prospects will offer objections to change in their buying patterns (as they are perhaps buying from competition). The sales person must be able to distinguish between valid and superficial objections. The most important plan of sales calls is the way calls should be closed with the prospect's purchase orders in hand.

Finally sales persons need to know how to arrange a post call analysis to learn the gains of the plans as well as its shortcomings.

Prospecting

Prospecting can be divided into four parts, the advantages of having a skilled salesperson in the technique of prospecting, learning the methods and sources for identifying and locating the worthwhile prospects, qualifying the prospects - by understanding the more desirable prospects from the less desirable one's, the relationship between prospecting and creative selling.

Every salesperson has to find new customer-the prospects. Customers are the existing buyers while prospects are likely buyers. Prospects can be considered as potential buyers of the company's products. Prospecting can be defined as" identifying and qualifying potential customers or prospects" salespersons need to learn the prospecting of potential customers to enable them to replace lost customers due to organisational changes, relocation, competitive activities. A skilled salesperson will be able to prioritise calls on prospects more likely to become customers, making the sales calls more productive. Such salesperson will be able to broad base his customer list and increase the total number of his customers. He will reduce the number of unproductive calls in the process.

Prospect Identification

In several product groups it is easy to identify the prospects, like the cotton supplier will know the textile mills as his prospects, the airlines would identify the travel agents as the prospects. However, for products with a large number of possible customers like insurance, office supplies it is more difficult to locate the prospects. In such cases, companies develop ingenious techniques for identifying the prospects. One insurance company's sales manual has a list of 140 different sources of prospects of life insurance. Published data, lists, telephone directories are good source of potential customers. Today's telemarketers use these lists for calling on the prospects to know their interest in the product being sold. Salespersons use referrals extensively for locating prospects. Company's existing customers are known to recommend another possible buyer to the salesperson. This can happen on the buyer's own volition or on salesperson's request. At times even prospects can give referrals of other prospects and the salesperson can use the Endless Chain of prospecting potential customers. Besides, influential business leaders, community leaders can become source of prospecting for customers. These influential persons are found at the centre stage of power. Even bankers, lawyers, educators can be used as such sources.

One major area that brings about prospects is the enquiries, (that could have been generated because of companies advertising efforts or sales promotion,) that the company receives from prospects. These enquiries are passes on to the salespersons as business leads.

Salespersons should always be on the alert for locating new customers-the companies prospects. It is a good idea to develop a data bank that is kept updated for the prospects by adding the prospects from all the possible sources.

Once the salesperson has got the name of the prospect his task actually starts. The salesperson must find out in the prospects organisation, the right person who should be met for business. Ideally the entire purchase decision hierarchy should be understood along with other particulars like phone, address, email address. A study confirms that 60 % of sales calls are made on wrong persons and are therefore ineffective. Sales calls are expensive as a lot of time is spent on planning and executing the calls. It is necessary that the time and effort are wisely invested. Salespersons should therefore, start with making calls on the best prospects, those whose chances of getting converted into customers are the best.

Qualifying the Customer

Qualifying helps the salesperson in selecting the best prospects on whom to call. The following three questions are used for qualifying the prospects:

1. Does the prospect meet with the company's policies?
2. Does the product fulfil a need of the prospect?
3. What is the current and future value of the prospect to the company?

In the case of company policy the salesperson should understand the prospects requirements on the following terms of business and the company's standards on the same:

1. Pricing and discounts

2. Credit as a sales tool
3. Cash discounts
4. Delivery needs
5. Order size
6. Servicing requirements.

Prospects with odd or abnormal requirements that the company cannot comply with is not a good prospect as against the prospect who requires only the standard terms of business. Such prospects are likely to offer long term business association to the company. The other, even more important question is, do company's product and service, including delivery periods fill the prospects needs? Prospects with urgent needs that can be met by the company have the best chance of becoming company's customers. However, in majority of cases the prospects do not see any need for the company's products in immediate future or even in the distant future. At such times it is the job of the salesperson to find out a way in which the company's product can satisfy some need of the prospect. It must be understood clearly that even if the prospect does not see any need of the company's product but the salesperson does see a need then the prospect is worth working on. A company modernising its plant will have need of a bigger, more powerful air conditioning system even if the company does not realise at the moment. It would be prudent for the salesperson to introduce his company's latest energy saving powerful air conditioning system when the buyer is in the right frame of mind to listen.

A napkin salesperson read in a magazine that one industrial laboratory had many delicate instruments that needed soft lint free cloth to wipe off dust from the instruments. While the purchase person of the laboratory may never have thought of buying napkins for the purpose, the alert salesperson saw the need and now that and similar several other laboratories are using the napkins.

Therefore, the salesperson should not get worried even if the prospect shows no interest in the product, and try to locate even hidden needs of which even the prospect is not aware.

The next level is to find out the present and future value of the prospect to the company. It stands to reason that the best efforts should be made on prospects with the greatest value to the company. The prospects capacity is one yardstick for measuring the value. The biggest buyer gets to be the best prospect. Big value frequent orders from the prospect make him most valuable. However, even a small buyer with future growth possibilities can never be ignored. Besides, the prospects reputation is a major factor in considering its value. A small buyer who is a community leader and much respected should be rated high on value even against the bigger volume buyers who may be poorly regarded in the business circles.

Summarising, the good prospect can be defined as the one that meets the business policy and terms of business of the company, has a definite need of the company's products and has a high present or future value for the company, or if the prospect enjoys leadership position in the industry or in the community.

So far a variety of techniques of prospecting have been studied. It is obvious that the prospecting techniques will differ greatly among the salespersons depending on the kind of selling job they are performing, the product. Prospecting for customers requires creative ability on the part of the salesperson. Salespersons creativity is perhaps the only limiting factor for developing prospecting plans for future customers. At the same time the creative salesperson can determine newer ways of product usage by the potential customers.

3.4 DETAILED CALL PLANNING

Salespersons need to learn in detail the various aspects of call planning before a call is made on a customer or a prospect. Sales calls are costly and time consuming both for the salesperson and the buyer, it is essential that the calls are planned in advance and thoroughly. Some salespersons feel that playing by the ear will take them through a successful sales call. However, experience shows that such calls usually end in disaster. Planning needs to be first perceived in the mind only. Planning process takes the salesperson through what will be done in future well in advance. The sales calls are important assignments and the risk of lack of preparedness must be avoided at all cost. A successful call could generate business worth millions of rupees as the reverse is equally true. Call planning needs to be done in the following three steps:

1. Establish the call objective
2. Gather the essential information
3. Select appropriate strategies or tactics.

Establishing the Call Objectives

The call objective is what the salesperson hopes to achieve when he meets the customer or the prospect face to face. The objective must be set before the call is made. Finally the objective that any salesperson has—is to obtain an order from the customer or the prospect. The objective may quantify the order value for the call. However, more often than not, it takes several calls before an order can be obtained. Therefore each call may have a different objective, while the major objective of obtaining the order is always at the back of the salesperson's mind. The immediate objective could be to find out changes in buying patterns with the change of purchase team of the customer. Other objective is to persuade the customer or prospect to see a product demonstration. One objective could be to obtain permission to supply samples for trial purposes. There can be a variety of objectives of sales calls and the calls can be considered as fruitful if the objective for the call has been met. In any case, since the final objective is getting the order, the other minor objectives should bring the main objective a little closer to the company. The objectives of preliminary calls should be used like the steps of an escalator that lead to the final destination, the order. The number of steps, or calls leading to the order would depend on the type of selling as also it will vary from customer to customer. Setting up objectives help the salesperson in keeping calls on track of achieving the main objective. For example, if the salesperson wants to introduce a new type of denim cloth to the manufacturer of ready made garments, the following route can be taken:

1. First objective—to get the agreement of the buyer about need of the denim
2. Second objective—demonstrate the new denim to key individuals
3. Convince the buyer that the price and other terms of business are right and get the order.

As can be seen the intermediate objectives were in line with the major objective of getting the order. The objectives must follow a sequence in ascending order like an escalator, as it will help the salesperson in getting the order rather quickly.

Gathering the Essential Information

Once the objective has been defined the next step is gathering essential information about the customer or the prospect. During the prospecting stage the salesperson has obtained some information. However, the more information he has the better chances of his success from the sales calls. While information gathering is time consuming it is important to collect the essential information.

The salesperson has to determine what constitutes the essential information on the prospect. It is the objective of the call that defines the information need of the salesperson. It is useful to prepare a check-list of information needs in order to avoid overlooking any necessary information item. Given below is a dedicated checklist, which should be altered by the salesperson to suit individual requirements-

Business Information Check List

1. Name
2. Address
3. Telephone numbers, Fax
4. Annual sales volume in rupees and units
5. Ownership
6. Management philosophy
7. Organisational structure
8. Key decision makers

9. Reputation
10. Competition details
11. Credit rating
12. Number of employees
13. Current problems faced by the company
14. Products/services sold
15. Markets targeted-segments
16. Key customers
17. Plans and policies on purchasing
18. Budget policy
19. Frequency of purchase
20. Seasonal factors
21. Key suppliers
22. Attitude towards price, quality, product innovations
23. Raw material used
24. Components made/bought
25. Manufacturing process
26. Administrative process
27. Machine and equipment used
28. Schedule of maintenance
29. Volume potential for sales by the salesperson in rupees and in numbers
30. Previous experience with the salesperson's company
31. Salesperson's competition

The check list of personal information

1. Name with correct spelling and pronunciation
2. Address
3. Age with date of birth
4. Position—title, responsibility, authority, line of communication, basis of evaluation by superiors
5. Length of time with the company
6. Business background
7. Education
8. Business or professional affiliations
9. Social affiliations
10. Marital status, family background and number of children
11. Other interests—outside of the job
12. Personal aspirations
13. Personal peculiarities

14. Best time to visit.

While several of the items listed may not be considered as essential, it is a good idea to go through the checklist to ensure nothing of vital importance is left out.

Salesperson need to know the sources from where they can gather the information. Information on existing customers is usually available with the salesperson's company. Besides, customers or prospects who give the business leads are another source of information. Trade partners, the channel members, trade publications. Business calls should be used to gain information that help in adding onto the already available information. Prospects annual reports, balance sheets reveal important details on their financial standing, plans and new product launches. Prospects product literature, advertisements offer information that can be of use to the salesperson. The salesperson should use all possible means to get the information and keep it updated all the time.

Strategies and Tactics

Salespersons must plan their strategies for the sales calls to attain their call objectives. The calls normally follow the following pattern:

1. Approach
2. Presentation
3. Objections
4. Closing the call

Due to the importance of sales calls, call planning must become an essential part of the salesperson's activities and it should become a work habit with the salesperson. Planning being a mental activity,should be carried out at a place where there are no distractions. Salesperson should concentrate on the three elements of call planning, establishing the objective, gathering the essential information and selecting the appropriate tactics. The planning can be done mentally. However, it is recommended that for important call the plan must be written down. Given below is a standard form for planning sales calls:

Call Planner

Company

Address

Phone, fax

Name of the customer/ prospect

Call objective

Essential information on the company-on the individual

Call planner -continued

Tactics to use

a. Approach

b. Presentation

c. Objections

d. Closing

It should be assumed that the customer is a busy person and when he gives an appointment for a sales call, it is important that the salesman makes the best use of the time given, and hence the need for careful planning for each such call.

Planning sales calls should be done using the following steps:

- Study the customer's file; remember the name (with correct pronunciation), designation, level and authority of the person to be met. Review of any complaint from the customer, whether it has been attended to, satisfactorily so far or not. Is there any pending matter from the last call, which must be resolved before the call is made, or else the salesman may not be even welcome at the customer's premises? For example if the salesman had promised replacement of defective product and it has not taken place so far, the sales call would end up in bitter criticism from the customer and undue justification from the salesman. No concrete result can come from such a situation.
- Plan the sales call objectives, both major and minor ones. It is better to write them down at least in first few calls.
- Carry the following in the briefcase to be used at the customers place
  a. Visiting cards
  b. Customer's file
  c. Product Literature, especially of new products being introduced
  d. Testimonials from other customers
  e. Firms letterheads
  f. Price lists
  g. Terms of business
  h. Pen, pencils, erasers, carbon paper, stapler with staples
  i. Products benefits for the customer along with benefits offered by competition (make sure your benefits always outscore the competitive benefits) the benefits should be written in sequence of their priority for the customer and it may be wise to alter the sequence for different levels of customers hierarchy.

The salesman should be smartly dressed and not gaudily and well groomed. In most cases it is essential to take prior appointment from the customer. It is useful to reach customer's office a few minutes early (while waiting the salesman can compose himself, revise the file papers, plan his opening sentences, use the toilet to feel fresh, comb his hair.)

In case of meeting a new customer, or one who has been mostly buying from competition dialogue plan, which has been found useful as at several steps the salesman is likely to find objections to his benefit story is given below. Of course the salesman must keep his wits about him to modify it as the sales call progresses.

The main objective of sales calls is getting the Purchase order from the customer. Salesmen usually plan a canned talk to persuade the customer to place the order on the salesman's firm. However, the salesman mostly, encounters resistance from the buyer due to the following reasons, one or all:

- The buyer is friendly to the competitors sales person
- Competitive product gives better value for money in the eyes of the buyer
- Competition provides better after sales service as per the buyer
- The users in the customer's side do not want a change, to avoid problems of duplicated inventories and confusion from unskilled/ illiterate workers about a new product
- The competition is providing some unspecified incentive, overtly or covertly to the buyer

Following are the steps needed in guiding the buyer in deciding in favour of placing the order on the firm. It is called the **Decision Triangle** (when more than one buying decision person are involved then the triangle could take the shape of **Decision Pyramid.)**

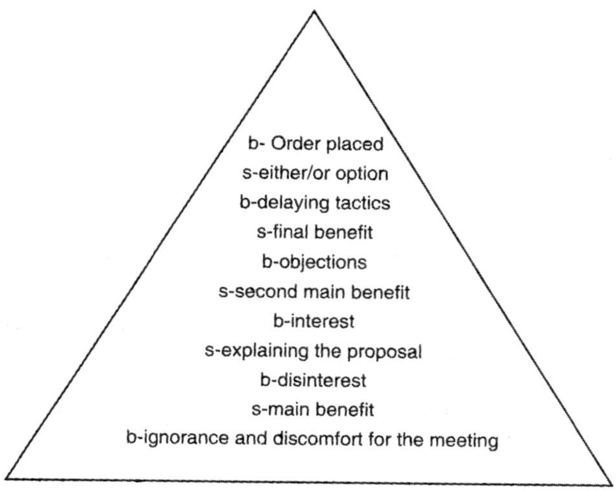

b-buyer, s-salesman

As can be seen in the beginning of the interview the salesman is at a disadvantage as the customer is ignorant of his proposal. At this juncture it is best to give the most important benefit, which would attract the attention of the buyer. If the benefit could be translated in to savings in rupees, it will click well with the CEOs, Finance Managers; time saving will go well with production managers. Even after the main benefit, the salesman need not feel complacent as the competitive strengths are still working to defuse their effort. At this stage the salesman must explain the proposal and if the buyer wants he can call other members of decision-making team to join him. It will save time for both seller and the buyer. Otherwise, similar dialogue will have to be carried out with other members separately. After some interest is generated the salesman would do well to seize the opportunity by adding the other benefits till the buyer reaches the stage of purchase decision. At times there is a last hurdle, which is basically a delaying tactic on the part of the buyer, like I have to consult my father (who may not be even involved in the business at all). This can be surmounted by offering an option to the buyer, "would you want us to provide the transit insurance or you would cover it yourself?" If the customer says, "we will take the insurance cover ourselves" your deal is finalized. Once the salesman gets the purchase order, he must make sure to thank the buyer and leave his office without delay. It has been known that if the salesman stays long enough he may lose the order, "could you just give me that order back for a minute I want it to be checked once more by our auditors" you hand over the order and can wish it good by as the next day the competitors salesman would walk in, get the benefit of your sales talk which has brought the buyer in to buying mood, and he will walk away with your order.

In case there is buying committee to take decisions the salesman can act as a liaison man by getting the following to meet and put across the benefit story as per the mindset and need of the member of the committee, thus the decision triangle becomes decision pyramid:

Firm's CEO with buyers CEO-this could perhaps be the last meeting unless of course the two CEOs know each other well.

Technical manager/R&D manager with the buyers R&D manager

Systems manager with buyers Production manager

Logistics manager with buyers Materials manager

Finance manager with buyers Finance manager

These meetings could be on one-to-one basis or altogether

Goals for Personal Selling

Call Planning Process

Note: In the following paragraphs the words used–Customer and Prospect are interchangeable.

a. Approach

Once the call planning is complete, the salesperson starts the necessary arrangements to make the presentation before the customer or the prospect.

This process is called approach that includes the purpose of approach and its definition. Besides the techniques of getting to see the prospect or the customer has to be learnt. The approach can be defined as the activity of the salesperson that begins with making arrangements to see the customer or the prospect and ends with the start of the presentation. The approach has three basic purposes:

1. To get to see the prospect or the customer
2. To put him in the right frame of mind for the presentation
3. To confirm the call plan.

The first activity is to make an appointment for visiting the customer or the prospect. These appointments are made on telephone or through letters depending on time available between call and the appointment. In certain cases where the salesperson has become familiar with the customer and knows his routine, he may not make an appointment. For major business deals appointments must be considered as essential. The timing of the call should be to the customer or prospects convenience. If no appointment has been made then the time the customer is usually free or the time he has kept for such meetings must be kept in mind. Many business deals have been lost due to wrong timing of the sales call.

For the meeting the salesperson must be decently dressed, polite in demeanour. He will, in all probability meet with the receptionist, or the secretary of the person he has to meet and the first impressions on these buffers must be perfect. These buffers usually screen the salesperson before he is allowed to meet the main person. Decent dress, courteous behaviour would do wonders in such cases. In case an appointment has not been taken these buffers can blackball the salesperson. In such cases the best way to gain the appointment is to use the reference of some important person known to the customer or the prospect. Visiting cards, brochures or other mailed material to the prospect can also be used to gain the appointment. At times when the visiting card is given to the buffer the salesperson can write a small note on it to improve his chances for the meeting. These buffers or intermediaries play an important role in the salesperson getting the appointment. These are the virtual gatekeepers and it is best to keep them on the salesperson own side. The fact that the competitors are also doing the same thing should spur the salesperson into making friends of the buffers. Sending greeting cards to the them, thank you notes and small gifts during festive periods will be of great help.

Most of the time the salesperson has to wait to meet the right person. The waiting time should be properly utilised by revising the presentation plans. The salesperson can try to obtain the essential information during the waiting time. The buffer may become a good source of such information. If none of these is possible the salesperson should keep some trade publications or other reading material to fully utilise the waiting time.

b. Presentation Ready

When the salesperson comes face to face with the customer, the first few minutes make the vital impact on whatever happens afterwards. The presentation success would largely depend on the frame of mind of the customer or the prospect. Following possibilities would prove the point:

1. The prospect has been extremely busy and is meeting the salesperson just out of courtesy.
2. The prospects company is passing through a minor crisis situation
3. The prospect has to rush out to meet some VIP
4. The prospect has to meet a deadline and he is already late.

The salesperson needs to keep a positive outlook in all such times and he can gradually convert the negative frame of mind into positive approach of the prospect. The salesperson should ensure that prospect does not consider himself obligated under some duress into meeting him. The prospect should be ready and willing to meet and this happens when the salesperson is ready to help, and remains positive during the meeting. The sincerity and helpful nature are the prerequisites of success in the meeting. A negative behaviour from the salesperson would surely evoke similar response from the prospect. At times the history of earlier calls comes as a barrier of positive outlook of the salesperson and brings in a feeling of inadequacy. Conversely a successful earlier call could make the salesperson over confident and aggressive. Salesperson's own business results can seriously affect his behaviour during the meeting. The maturity of the salesperson is in throwing off or ignoring these factors that tend to influence his behaviour.

The salesperson has to take each call as a fresh experience. The vital matter is of attitude the salesperson must have, and that should be positive and helpful towards the prospect. The attitude will help the salesperson in getting the prospect into transitional mode where the buyer's mind is gently moved from whatever he had been doing prior to the salesperson's meeting to an enthusiastic willingness to hear the presentation. The salesperson needs to build a good rapport with the prospect. Rapport is defined as a "harmonious relationship". The rapport can be built by even small things like knowing the title, and the correct pronunciation of his name. Small talk, like talk about his hobbies, sports or other non business subjects in which the prospect is genuinely interested will contribute to the rapport building exercise. However, the small talk bit must be kept small since the prospect would not want to waste his valuable time. The salesperson should also make the best usage of the meeting time. Once the rapport has been established the Salesperson has to bridge the gap between the social conversation and the specific business of the call. A variety of techniques are used for bridging the gap as given below:

1. At times a question is asked for the purpose. "If I can show you how to reduce maintenance cost by 5%, would it be interest to you? " is such a question.

2. The other method could be of offering assistance, "I would like to check your air conditioning system for the coming summer. Of course there will be no charge"
3. Announcing a significant fact can be used to bridge the gap like," you will be happy to learn that since last December the Electricity supply company is saving rupees fifty lacs
4. Each year with the use of computerised billing system supplied by us
5. Sometimes the product like a miniature cell phone needs to be shown for bridging the gap.

The salesperson should always avoid such trite questions, "how is business" or "how do things look". Such questions are likely to get a negative response leading to the entire presentation becoming negative from the prospect viewpoint. The other failed technique is, "I was in the neighbourhood and thought I would drop in". Summarising after the rapport has been built the salesperson needs to have a technique of bridging the gap between the social conversation and serious business talk.

Call Plan Verification

Call planning involves the three steps, establishing the objective, gathering essential information and selecting the right tactics. The salesperson believes that his objectives are attainable, information sufficient and tactics appropriate. However, it is a good idea to verify the plan if the opportunity for doing so presents itself. The verification becomes easy if the prospect is given full rein to talk fully and openly. Salesperson needs to ask a well worded question after the gap has been bridged between the small talk and serious business talk leading to the presentation. Questions like, "your new plant installation plan?" Or "your maintenance plan for the machinery"—would let the prospect hold the fort and he would enjoy talking about his ideas. The salesperson could ask, "which part of the machinery is difficult to maintain?" or "which is the most time consuming manual operation that you want transferred to a computer?" the purpose of these questions is to have the prospect talk about his needs. The talks should be carried on till the call plan has been verified by the salesperson. The questions should be broad based to allow a general response. The salesperson should keep showing his interest by interjecting with, "this is interesting, tell me more". Attentive listening will help the salesperson in his verification process of the call plan. If the salesperson feels he can modify the plan as he goes along. He can decide if the original objective is still attainable or should he modify it to an extent. He would also realise if he has sufficient essential information or he should let the prospect keep talking. He can also understand if his tactics will work or do they need to be altered too. Can he use the tactics in handling the objections and in closing the presentation? The verification is the last step before the salesperson begins the presentation. As he is verifying his information base, the salesperson should help the prospect in redefining his needs from being generic to the needs of salesperson products through persuasive communication.

Sales Presentation for Customers—Process of Personal Selling

The salesperson has by now understood that unless he has a defined objective, essential information and planned the right tactics, he should not even attempt the call on the prospect. The start of the call is when the salesperson, through his persuasive communication gets the prospect change his generic needs to specific needs of the salespersons products. Let us discuss the persuasive communication in some detail.

The salesperson's products have some inherent unique qualities that can be defined as Product Features. Features need not be restricted to product physical qualities alone. They could well be part of company policy, product availability, and related service. Country wide advertising campaign would be part of company marketing policy. When the salesperson helps the distributor in managing the inventory the service offered is unique and personal. Each company has to provide proper training to its salesperson in understanding its product's unique qualities including the service and the marketing policy. Salespersons must keep themselves abreast on these counts.

The salesperson must understand that the customers buy a product only for the benefits it offers to them. Benefits can be defined as the satisfaction, the product provides to the buyers. The prospects are going to buy a product only if provides the needed benefit to them. Youngsters do not buy motor cycles; they buy the thrill they provide on high speeds. Women do not buy cosmetics; they buy the benefit of becoming alluring by using the same. However, different people are looking for different types of benefits from a product.

The salesperson therefore needs to list down the benefits different persons are looking from their product. Such a list needs to be continuously updated for each group of customers as the customer group keeps changing; market segment keeps changing with time. In early 1960s the transistor radio was the craze with the elite of the society and today they would feel ashamed if found near a transistor set. The benefits could include reduced cost of labour, reduced maintenance cost, better quality control and increased worker safety. For retail traders the benefits could be better protection from competitive actions, increased stock turnover, higher margins, less customer returns and complaints. A description of the product features would appear like a technical manual only. Likewise if the salesperson talks only about the benefits it would sound like parrot repeating what he has been taught. Persuasive communication should combine the two, with salesperson talking about the benefits along with the features from where the benefits are derived. Automatic transmission is a feature of some cars while convenience is the benefit to the car driver. Hence, if the salesperson tells the customer that with automatic transmission of our cars, you would find driving convenient and pleasurable, he is trying a feature with a benefit. For excelling in this type of communication the salesperson should prepare a Feature-Benefit worksheet, as given below:

Feature Benefit Worksheet

For -product-customer

Feature 1	Benefit 1	Benefit 2	Benefit 3	Benefit 4
Feature 2	Benefit 1	Benefit 2	Benefit 3	Benefit 4
Feature 3	Benefit 1	Benefit 2	Benefit 3	Benefit 4
Feature 4	Benefit 1	Benefit 2	Benefit 3	Benefit 4

Maslow's Hierarchy of needs gives a clear definition of different types of human needs and the salesperson would do well in relating the benefits to the needs, like physiological needs, need for safety, social acceptance need, need for recognition and respect and finally need for self actualisation, when the customer has attained the heights he had planned to achieve. It is assumed in the above worksheet that each feature will have multiple benefits.

Given below is a Feature Benefit Worksheet for a car:

Features	Benefits
Big seats	Comfort and lifestyle
Leg room, head clearance	Comfort and lifestyle
Large Boot	Family luxury car
Power steering	Lifestyle
Plush finish	Self actualised owner
Country wide service facility	Peace of mind –comfort
Easy payment plan	Economical
Exchange facility	Easy on budget, economical
Test drive possible	Reconfirmation of quality, lifestyle
Service pickup and delivery	Comfort
50 years experience	Peace of mind, lifestyle

Before the salesperson starts his presentation, he should have developed the feature benefit worksheet. The features should be first listed and then the benefits added on to the worksheet. In case of a car, the benefits can be listed as given below:

1. Comforts
2. Economy
3. Prestige enhancing lifestyle
4. Convenience
5. Safety

The salesperson should develop the Benefit Story using the possible benefits and writing down a paragraph for each benefit that will help him during the presentation, as given below-

Benefit Paragraph

Comfort

It is a comfortable car. The body is welded. The ride is so smooth you can pour tea or coffee from the jug and it will not spill. The large seats will take a well fed family of six and the leg room ensures comfortable seating for the long legged teenagers.

The large boot is much bigger than several cars with big boots. You can really load it up without damage to your luggage or to the car.

It is a comfortable car for you, your family and your luggage.

Economy

The car costs less to run. The engine is newly designed for maximum efficiency. It is made out of aluminium to save weight. As a result you get up to 20 kilometres per litre. It is a real miser with petrol.

You can see the engine is uncluttered. It results in time saving for quick adjustments.

The body is welded, which means no rattle repairs. Its rustproof too, it will stand up to all weather.

The aluminium silencer will last twice as long as the ordinary one. The finish stays shiny so you save on waxing the car.

If you have a car to trade in, we will give a fair trade — in allowance, through our used car department.

You just cannot beat the economy of this model.

Prestige Enhancer-Lifestyle Product

It is a modern car. The new engine-101 horsepower will let you climb hills as though they were not there. Cruising speed in this model will leave you with plenty to spare for passing on motor ways. You will not find a welded body like this even in the best imports of sports cars and the design and the gleaming finish makes it unusually attractive. Of course you get power steering, power breaks and automatic transmission to give the ride you will enjoy.

Convenience

The car makes driving easier and its uncluttered engine makes maintenance simpler too. It is, as can be seen 184” long and can be parked in places smaller than ever before for other cars. The car provides spare space in the garage.

The boot will easily hold enough luggage for the long trips planned in the new car. The finish is a cinch to keep glistening clean; only a cold water wash does it quickly.

For ease of driving, parking and safety the car has power steering, power brakes and automatic transmission.

For periodic maintenance checkups and adjustments, there is complete modern service department at your disposal. If you like you can call me and will personally make arrangements for your service appointments. Should you need servicing in out of town locations in the country we have provided with a list of our numerous authorised service stations in the country along with a route maps so that you can never miss them. We have an easy payment plan so that you can keep your savings in the bank.

I would like to take you out on a test drive to show you how easy the car is to drive, first hand.

Safety

It is a solid car. These are real doors and the engine is placed up front for balance and greater control. You see the engine is V form and it gives a lower bonnet for battery visibility. The welded body gives you a substantial and strong car that takes all kinds of road punishments. Seat belts in rear seats are big safety plus in the car. You can rely on us to stand by the car. I have been selling cars for this dealer for the last fifteen years and hope to be here for another fifteen.

As can be seen from the benefit paragraphs that all the benefits from different features on comfort have been listed at one place. Similarly the other list of benefits is used to form sentences in the proper sequence for highlighting the benefits. Once the benefit story has been developed the next step is to find techniques for Maintaining Interest of the prospect.

Maintaining Interest

Salesperson's presentations are in many ways like telling a story. An interesting story is easy to listen while the same is not true for a boring story. Therefore, the next element of persuasive communication is maintaining the interest of the prospect. There are a number of techniques of maintaining the prospects interest as given below:

Customising or Individualising the Benefits

This means that the salesperson directs everything he says towards the needs of the prospect he is facing. This is important because each prospect wants to know how the product will satisfy his specific needs. Such individualisation of benefits will ensure that prospect's interest is maintained. It must be understood that two prospects buying identical product may be motivated by different benefits. Car buyers may have different motivations as one may buy a car for its economy and the other for its convenience. Individualising the needs and benefits means selecting those benefits that would satisfy the need of a particular prospect. Hence the salesperson would have to scan the benefit paragraphs that are ideally suited to the prospects requirements. In other words the salesperson must develop a storehouse of all possible features/ benefit stories to be able to build instant rapport and continued interest in the presentation by the prospect. The right selection of the benefit paragraph could mean success of the presentation and in obtaining the objective of the call.

Using Descriptive Language

The other method of maintaining the prospects interest is using descriptive language. For example, the car salesperson while using the comfort paragraph, does not just say that the car ride will be smooth, he says, "the ride will be so smooth you can pour coffee" the vivid language helps in maintaining the prospects interest. In the economy paragraph, the salesperson says "the car is real miser on petrol" he is using the descriptive language to hold interest of the prospect. A good salesperson is ready with descriptive language that he has developed with practice and he uses it to good advantage to keep the interest of the prospect.

Participation

The salesperson can keep the interest of the prospect alive if he, instead of relating his benefit story even when the prospect is getting bored with it. Participation means getting him involved in the act. This can be done in the following ways:

Ask the prospect a question, which will ensure his active participation in the presentation. The salesperson can ask, "Do you recall the trouble you had during your last trip in your car?"

Have the prospect do some calculating or figuring out, which would involve him in the presentation. The prospect can be asked to calculate the kilo metres per litre the car will give by giving him some documented figures.

For communicating persuasively the salesperson has to ensure that the prospect remains interested in the presentation, which he can do by individualising the benefits for prospects needs, keep his language descriptive, and ensure prospect's participation.

Believability

The fifth element of persuasive communication is its believability. Unless the prospect believes in the salesperson, the call can never be successful. One basic technique used by salesperson for ensuring the believability factor with the prospect is the use of testimonials. Testimonials are stories of satisfied customers that are most helpful for new products or when you are calling on a prospect. A testimonial issued by a reputed and respected company or person in the same field, help in convincing the prospect of the desirability of the product. Salespersons with thorough knowledge of product features and the benefits sought by the prospect can also make a believable presentation. His knowledge should be so extensive and exhaustive that he is able to politely answer all the questions asked by the prospect and give his benefit story convincingly. In the event the salesperson does not know the answer to a question it is best to admit it and confirm that in a day or two he will give the answer, instead of bluffing his way. Any wrong statement made is going to have a snowballing effect and the chances are that the prospect will soon become disillusioned with the salesperson and his presentation. The third technique for creating believability in the prospect results from the demeanour of the salesperson. It is easier to believe a sincere person. The salesperson should try to take the role of a personal counsellor to the prospect. He needs to under claim and over achieve the key points of his presentation. This way he will achieve the believability factor from the prospect.

Summarising there are three methods of achieving believability of the prospect, use of testimonials, having a thorough knowledge of product features and benefits and the salesperson's sincerity towards the prospect.

Demonstration

At times words are just not enough for achieving though call objective as the words appeal only to the prospect's sense of hearing. The other four senses are therefore neglected. We come to the sixth element of persuasive communication-demonstration. Demonstration means appealing to prospect's other sense to make the verbal presentation more persuasive. Demonstration in selling is basic. It is better for the buyer to enjoy chocolate slab rather than someone telling him how good it tastes. The housewife would rather feel the sari fabric than have a TV commercial describe how it feels.

Selling to the channel member, the retailer, if the salesperson does not describe the new advertising campaign but actually shows him the print copy.

A computer buyer would like to have hands on experience on the new model rather than only descriptive eulogy on the same. Buyers of air conditioning plant would be happy to visit an existing installation of the salespersons company and see for themselves the efficacy of the plant.

Salesperson has to decide what needs to be demonstrated and what need not be demonstrated. This requires a careful study of the Benefit Paragraphs. Statements that can be strengthened through an appeal to the other four senses should be carefully considered. Demonstrations make the features and benefits more believable. With some originality, zest and excitement can be added with the demonstration making the presentation more interesting.

Sellers of stainless steel products offer a key chain to the buyer as a proof of its rust proofing feature to increase the believability of the presentation.

Pictures of beautifully constructed villas can add the believability factor for the real estate salesperson.

With the huge dispersion of TV network in the country demonstration has become easy. Functions of an air compressor, farm equipment, dumpers, can be easily demonstrated on TV. In markets, the advertising vans help in demonstrating the products with the use of audio-visual equipment.

Demonstration that can involve the prospect's active participation will help in maintaining his interest. You must have noticed the detergent advertisements where the group of housewives are asked to join in the actual process of using the detergent. It is a good idea to indirectly demonstrate the service facilities the company has, by showing their pictures and a map where dotted locations of the facilities have been marked.

Demonstrations make features and benefits more understandable and believable. If they are original they make presentation more interesting. If the demonstration requires the use of physical materials like, OHP, LCD Projector, charts the salesperson must ensure that the materials and the equipment are in good working order and that the salesperson has personally used it several times. If the salesperson was to fumble through the demonstration the prospect will lose confidence. Therefore, all the equipment must be thoroughly checked before each call. Smooth demonstration would increase the believability of the presentation.

Planning Presentations for Specific Calls

Salesperson should list down the key elements of the presentation, the product features, benefits to stress, the technique of maintaining interest and achieving believability. Appeals to the other four senses that the salesperson plans to use must also be noted. The features and the benefits must be individualised for the prospect on each call. The demonstration planned must also be tailor-made for each prospect. The lap top computer salesperson gave a hands on demonstration to the users of the prospects company, talked about the economies in usage with the prospect's Finance Director and gave the benefit story highlighting the latest features to the CEO. A good presentation converts the need to desire through persuasive communication. Individualised demonstration makes the presentation more effective.

c. Handling Objections

As the salesperson makes his presentation towards achieving his call objectives, the prospect is likely to make statements detrimental to the achievement of objectives. These statements can be defined as objections. The salesperson must realise that these are normal parts of every sales call and should not be discouraged by them. In fact they may reveal new information that will help you to adjust your tactics. Realistically, therefore, objections should be considered as not deterrents in achievement of objectives but they may serve to help you in readjusting your sales tactics.

The following five steps need to be considered for handling objections—

The **first step** is listening to the prospect. The salesperson must train himself in the art of listening carefully to the objections raised by the prospects. Salespersons have a tendency to talk rather than to listen. A quiet and patient listener may find the prospect himself talking out of the objection. The prospect must be encouraged to speak uninterruptedly and the salesperson may get to know some additional information that he reveals, which could be of help to the salesperson. The prospect's manner of expressing the objection may confirm his personal negative feelings. The salesperson should not just listen to the words being spoken but also note the manner in which they are expressed. This way he will understand if the prospect has negative feelings as well as he may get some new information.

The **second step** is classifying the objections. Objections can be classified as valid or invalid. Let us consider the invalid objections. An objection is considered as invalid, when there is a concealed reason for it. Actually the prospect covers up how he feels by saying something else and hence should not be taken literally. A reluctance to make purchase decision could be the concealed or underlying reason behind the stated invalid objection. If the prospect says, "I cannot afford it just now, see me in a month" there may be an invalid objection as the prospect cannot say he is unable to decide at the present time. The other concealed reason for an invalid objection could be an aversion to change on the part of the prospect. "Regarding your product I will have to talk to my partner′ the prospect may be concealing his reason for buying your product since he has been buying from his present supplier for the past seven years. A prospect may raise an invalid objection if the salesperson has said something or done something to antagonise him. Hard selling on the part of salesperson may offend some prospect. A flippant or derogatory made unwittingly byte salesperson on some favourite project of the prospect could antagonise the prospect. An invalid objection is only a subtle front for a concealed, underlying reason for the prospect's objection.

As the invalid objections are now understood, let us study the valid objections. A valid objection can be taken literally, as the prospect means exactly what he says. For example if the prospect does not understand a technical point made by the salesperson he may raise a valid objection. "The new product is made of 16 gauge steel rather than 18 gauge" if the prospect does not know that the lower the gauge the thicker the steel, he may say, "I do not want something that is flimsy in construction". A valid objection may also be raise if the salesperson fails to stress the feature or the benefit of primary interest to the prospect. In case the buyer is especially interested in the construction of the product and the salesperson keeps emphasising on low price, he is stressing the wrong benefit.

Valid objections occur most frequently during the presentation.

Handling Objections Details

After the first part is over, that of listening and understanding valid and invalid objection, the next step is disarming. As you meet an objection you are faced with a disagreement. It is best to show consideration for the other person's viewpoint as follows:

1. One popular and effective method is, "yes but" method and it is meant to show consideration to the other person's point of view.
2. Other way of showing consideration is "that is an interesting observation"
3. Or "I am glad you brought it up"
4. And yet again, "yes I know how you feel, but"

As you show consideration for the prospect's viewpoint, you are in fact avoiding confrontation and arguments. Disarming prevents objections from developing into arguments between the prospect and the salesperson.

Once the salesperson has understood the techniques of listening, classifying and disarming it is time to understand the subject of answering the prospect's objections. Let us take the invalid objections first. For invalid objections the salespersons can use a number of answers like giving a token answer. For example, if the prospect says, "I am too busy right now" the salesperson can say disarmingly, "yes sir, everybody is busy these days but let me tell you...."

The other way of handling invalid objection is to ignore it completely by pausing and then continuing. The salesperson can divert the prospects attention away from the objection by bringing up some other interesting fact instead of handling the invalid objection directly. If the classification of the objection as invalid is correct it will not recur. If the prospect says, "business is terrible", disarmingly the salesperson can reply, "things are pretty tough, but a few moments ago we agreed that our new machine would...."

While answering valid objections it was agreed that they need to be taken on their face value. One other technique is, "denial" that may be used to answer valid objections. The best time to use denial is when the objections are based on misunderstanding or misinterpretation of the salesperson's facts. Suppose the prospect says, "I am not interested in the sweaters as they are made of reconditioned wool" knowing that the label clearly shows that the product is 100% virgin wool, disarming the salesperson can say, "yes sir, I am glad you brought it up; the quality of wool is most important, but all our sweaters are made of 100% virgin wool. Let me show you how we clearly mark the fact on our label".

Another example is, when the prospect says, "I am not buying now, times are too uncertain" the answer given disarmingly can be, "yes sir, but, among the certainties is a steady rise in cost of living and prices generally. You should protect yourself to a reasonable degree".

Next, the valid objections can be handled using the YIELD technique. It is used most frequently to overcome objections based on an existing advantage offered by the competition. The success of yield technique depends on the salesperson's ability to offset the existing benefit offered by the competition. For example, if a doctor says, "your capsules are larger than those supplied by your competitor. "The salesperson's response should be," yes doctor, our capsule is larger but, it is especially designed for ease of swallowing".

In case you are uncertain if the objection is valid or not, the best way out is ask, "why? " The why question will give the salesperson the necessary information to decide whether to classify the objection as valid or as invalid. For example if the prospect say, "I want to look into some other offers". The salesperson can say, disarmingly, "yes, but why would you want to look into other deals now?" the answer should help the salesperson determine if the objection is valid or not.

So far the discussion on answering objections has been on, listening, classifying, disarming and yielding. The last manner of answering the objections is that of continuing the presentation. After answering the prospects objection, you should continue with the presentation. Otherwise, the prospect will feel he has to raise another objection. The direction of the presentation will depend on what the salesperson has learned from the objection. Suppose the prospect revealed a particular concern about his company's service, the salesperson should stress on those special features of his company's service that were left out in the answers to the objection.

Summarising, the salesperson well versed with the storehouse of benefit paragraphs will be able to adept his presentation in response to the reactions of the prospect. The salesperson must continue his presentation as he reinforces the answers to the objection. It will prevent the objection from recurring later in the call.

Price Objection

After understanding the five ways of dealing with valid objections, let us consider a special case of valid objection, the price objection. The price objection is being handled separately because it is the one that plagues the salesperson most and is most difficult to handle. The price objections are of two types, "I cannot afford it" or, "I can get it for less".

The first type of price objection, "I cannot afford it" can be said as, "your price is too high", or "I cannot spend that much" or yet another, "I am looking for a cheaper product".

The salesperson's response in such cases can be, staring with denial, "yes sir, money is important, but, in the long run your savings will far outweigh this additional expenditure".

Normally the price objection is raised when the prospects knows that he can get the same product for a different price. If the salesperson knows his product has as higher price than the competitive product it is best to use the yield technique. Disarmingly the salesperson can say, "Yes our price is Rs.150 and competitive price is Rs. 125, but, the difference of Rs. 25 is eliminated by the one year free service contract we are offering that the competition does not. You will agree that one year fee service is definitely more than Rs 25. It is best to talk about the small difference and justify it rather than talk about the main price amount.

d. Call Closing

Call closing can be defined as a direct attempt on the part of the salesperson to attain the objective of the call. Let us, therefore discuss the techniques the salesperson can use to obtain his call objective. At this point you may be wondering if the salesperson knows his objective, makes a good approach, gives an effective presentation, and handles objections skilfully, it should be sufficient to attain the call objectives. The problem arises because most persons are reluctant to take decisions especially if they involve spending money. Salesperson's good approach, effective presentation, skilful handling of objections normally moves the prospect to the verge of agreement with the objective. However, the reluctance may still remain. Closing techniques are, therefore, direct attempts by the salesperson to nudge the fully persuaded prospect to make as favourable decision.

The first closing technique can be called assumptive. The assumptive technique is used when the salesperson senses that the buyer is almost at the point of making a decision in favour of the objective and has met with little resistance. When the salesperson is using the assumptive technique he does nothing more than act as though a favourable decision has been made with respect to the call objective. A machine tool salesperson, whose call objective was to arrange for the buyer to visit nearby plant in order to see the machine in operation, uses the assumptive technique. Sensing the favourable decision, he says, "let me use your phone to tell them we will be over there this afternoon" the salesperson has assumed that the favourable decision has been taken.

Another closing technique is of giving choice to the prospect. The technique is used when the salesperson senses that the buyer is close to agreement with his call objective but there still remains some resistance. The choice technique is a direct way of asking the prospect to make a favourable decision. In using the technique the salesperson gives the prospect a choice between two buying alternatives. The prospect does not have to select between order or no order, he has a choice between something and another thing. A shirt salesperson saying, "Would you buy the green shirt" leaves the option of saying no and walking out. Once the salesperson knows that the prospect is nearly ready to decide in favour of his objective, he could say, "which one should I pack, the green or the light blue one?" the moment the prospect says the blue one, you have achieved your objective. In B-to-B sales, the question that can be asked just before the final decision could be, "you would like us to arrange for transit insurance or would you like to organise it?"

In another situation where installation and commissioning of a plant is involved, the salesperson can nudge the prospect into decision by saying," should I send my installation team next week or would you prefer earlier."

Suppose the salesperson is selling room airconditioners and for nudging the prospect into action says," so it is the two ton one you will buy" he may get an answer, "NO". After sensing that the decision is near in his favour he should say," 1.5 ton or 2 ton, which is the one", and the chances are he will get the order for one of them.

The choice technique should be used when the salesperson has sensed that the decision in his favour is almost reached to help the prospect feel happier as he gets the last word and psychologically mastery over the salesperson. Anyway, you have achieved the call objective.

The third closing technique is the Summary technique. This technique is used in conjunction with the choice technique after several features and benefits have been emphasised. The salesperson should summarise using those features and benefits that have stimulated the greatest desire in prospects mind. In this technique the salesperson uses the summary as he reviews the features and benefits putting them in a capsule form." Your interest in economy and convenience will be fully realised by our low rate contract, our quality maintenance service and our low cost spare parts. The summary technique is best used along with the choice technique.

The fourth closing technique is named the Special Feature Technique. The features of a product have been defined earlier as unique qualities of the product. Sometimes, one of the features of the product may be used as closing technique to bring about favourable decision. If a product is in limited supply, it becomes its special feature. "These imported hoses do not come for the next six months. Shall I book hundred for you: "Prospects take favourable decision because they do not want to lose out on anything.

The favourable feature technique should be used only when the salesperson is sure of his facts and with utmost care. Dishonest or short-sighted approach is absolutely not recommended.

Timing

As the salesperson learns about the closing techniques where a nudge is required to gain the call objective, it is a good idea to learn how to sense the right time when the prospect has been persuaded enough and his desire to buy has reached the peak. The timing gives the salesperson the clue when to use the closing technique. If the salesperson delays too long before using the closing technique, the prospect may make a favourable decision on his own. This may be all right except too much time has gone into the presentation. If the closing technique is used prematurely he may cause an objection to be raised. When the prospect is not fully convinced he needs a nudge to help him take a favourable decision. Therefore, proper timing will help the salesperson to attain hic call objective quickly as well as to avoid objections. Prospects indicate through various means that their interest and desire are at a peak and they are ready for a favourable decision. The salesperson must be alert to the dues or the signs that tell that the right time to use the closing technique has come.

Sometimes the dues are obvious like the prospect asking, how soon can he get the samples? The salesperson should know that this is the right time to use the closing technique. The salesperson should reply, "In two days, shall I deliver it to you or have them mailed?" The salesperson is using the choice technique of call closing.

Another example of obvious clue is when the prospect says, "Can the survey be done after working hours?" The salesperson reply should be, "certainly, I will have our engineer in at 5 pm tomorrow" once the clues are seen the salesperson should move quickly to close the call.

However, the clues normally are not so obvious. The salesperson should be alert to recognise the subtle clues like a smile of agreement or a nod other mention of a specific feature or benefit. Understanding the subtle clue the salesperson should use the losing technique. Prospect may start examining the sales aid and start some figure work, examine his stock he is on the verge of a favourable decision and the time is ripe for using the closing technique.

Summarising, the salesperson should be alert to understand the obvious and also the subtle clues given by the prospect and that is the time for the use of closing technique.

Departure

The next step of the call is the departure and there are a few rules for an effective departure. At the end of the call, either the salesperson has attained his objective or he has not achieved it. In either case he must make an effective departure.

In case the objective has been achieved the salesperson should reassure the prospect that he has made a wise decision. Most people want such a reassurance. "Your decision to renew your service contract with us was an intelligent one that will mean continuous economies for your organisation" once the reassurance has been given it is best to leave quickly. Lingering on is not business like. Thank for the order and leave quickly is a golden rule. If a good rapport has been built a referral can be obtained before leaving.

However, if the objective has not been achieved remember the minor objective that keeps the door open and at least achieve it. The minor objectives should all be in line with the major call objectives, like, "when do you it would be appropriate for me to contact you again". Or "we are organising a seminar. / an exhibition and I would like to personally invite you for the same." As he gains the minor objective his feeling of disappointment will vanish and he will be ready for the next call in a positive frame of mind. The minor objective may ultimately lead the salesperson in achieving the major objective sooner than the salesperson can imagine. It is difficult to realise that the customer would get disillusioned with his existing supplier and that would be time he will think of you if you have left a good favourable impression on him. The salesperson should appreciate that while the main objective has not been attained, the minor objective has been achieved, as well as more information has been gathered about the prospect's company as well as about the prospect himself, that will be useful in future calls.

Post Call Analysis

After completing the call it is necessary to analyse the call just completed. The analysis starts with comparing the result of the call with the established call objective. The comparison will help the salesperson to plan his next call on this prospect. If the sales objective of the call has been achieved the salesperson can consider the manner in which the next call plan to escalate the prospect up towards some long range goal. If the objective was not attained the salesperson should critically review to determine the cause of failure, starting from the formulation of the call objective, was it too ambitious, too broad or, perhaps too specific. The salesperson should take a look at the essential information gathered before making the call. Were there gaps in the information, and how serious were they?

Next he should analyse the tactics used. Were the techniques used either in approach, presentation, handling of objections or closing inadequate? Were they the cause of his failure to attain the objective of the call?

Summarising the salesperson should review the three steps the salesperson had taken in planning the call as follows:

1. Establish the call objective
2. Gather the essential information
3. Select appropriate tactics

Only after such a critical review should the salesperson plan his next call on the same prospect.

Post call analysis serves a primary purpose of providing a sound basis for planning the next call on the prospect. Post call analysis can serve a secondary, broader purpose of helping the salesperson in his personal development. In other words, post call analysis should point out some of the strengths and weaknesses in the salesperson's overall performance which should go beyond this one call. The salesperson must accept the primary responsibility for the call failure and use the post call analysis for improving his call planning. For example, did the post call review reveal a growing deficiency in some aspects of product knowledge, or weakness in a special skill such as group presentation? Did the call analysis, instead prove the existence of some new fund strengths in handling people or in thinking creatively?

Summarising, post call analysis and personal development go hand in hand. The salesperson who uses each call experience for the purpose of personal improvement will move more rapidly toward a higher level of effective sales performance.

3.5 DEFINING SALES OBSTACLES

Following are the major obstacles that a salesperson faces during making a sale-

Habit—the customer is in the habit of using competitive product or service and finds it difficult to change

Fear—the customer fears the unknown and has unwarranted feeling of impending trouble of risk or of loss that confuses his thinking and causes him to evade opportunities that help him to maximise his capabilities.

Price—the customer fails to see the benefits that outweigh their money value

Complaint—the customer voices or feels dissatisfaction on the company's product or service.

Detail—the customer believes that the trouble that he has to take in buying the product is not worth the effort.

Lack of information—sales progress gets impeded when the salesperson has not informed the customer either due to his own lack of knowledge on the same or when the customer lacks the technical skills to understand the sales talk. At times the customer could be lacking in imagination to visualise the benefits of the product or even when the salesperson's expressions are unclear and confusing.

Competition—the customer believes that the competitive benefits would be more suited to him.

It must be understood that at times companies face competition from dissimilar things like a housewife may choose a new cooking range over a new washing machine.

Friendship-competition — the customer likes or respects competitive sales or other personnel or when the customer or the prospect believes that the competitive product will produce equal or greater amount of benefits to him.

Difficult personality—the prospect lacks emotional control and he allows the difference of opinion to degenerate or he indulges in temper, rudeness or other unwarranted behaviour that retards progress towards sales.

Time—customer feels that the company's product does not merit the time to be spent on its purchase, or if the sales call is made too late and yet any further postponement would cause failure of the talks or if the delivery requirements of the customer are urgent and cannot be met.

Release—the prospect wants a release from further discussion of the subject.

Divided release—the prospect wants release as he sincerely or insincerely says he has to discuss the matter with someone not present.

Negative mood or manner—salesperson's talk is creating through his frame of mind, manner of speaking and acting unfavourable reaction in the prospects mind causing dislike and lack of respect.

Poor judgement—when the salesperson does not care for the following-

- Prevailing conditions
- Comparing and separating right ways of doing things from wrong ways
- Planning the sales call- when to call, what to say and what to do.
- Deciding how to use the product benefits in the talk from the customers' viewpoint.
- Noting the effect on the customer on what is said or done.
- Keeping control of emotions
- Using knowledge of human nature and practical selling methods secured through study, analysis and experience.

3.6 COUNTERING THE OBSTACLES

Benefit—describe any good result, the customer will get from putting a good quality of the product to use.

Good quality—describe clearly the inherent trait or characteristic of the product or proposition or specific parts that make it possible to produce benefits when put to use.

Poor quality—clearly but tactfully describe traits and characteristics of an alternate product (competitive), that make it produce losses when put to use.

Loss—describe the losses poor quality will bring ever so subtly.

Proposition— inform the prospect the salesperson's name, company's name, brand, price, terms of business, delivery time.

Prestige—clearly describe the reputation and achievements of his company, its personnel, its products, services, and the customers, endorsers who lend their support.

Personal prestige—inform the prospect of the salesperson's accomplishments, experience and good reputation that creates a feeling of respect and confidence in the prospect.

Pride—inform the prospect of the respect he enjoys with the salesperson by stating his achievements, his company's accomplishments, or by asking his advice on some matter that he can comment on.

Assurance—use any combination of words to qualify the above stated counters with tactful directness or that has power to calm or reassure the prospect.

Story—give an account of an event that indirectly informs the prospect of reasons, emotions or both that help him in deciding in the salesperson's favour.

Good turn—salesperson should perform or offer to perform any good turn that has power to build liking and respect and which places the prospect under no obligation.

Contact—classify the business or personal friendship between the salesperson and the prospect and mention friends, hobbies, other outside activities that establish common interests.

Explanation—make the meaning of technical terms used by classifying words and use similes, demonstrations, charts, presentations. photographs to clarify details of an operation.

Mood and manner—salesperson's frame of mind, manner of speaking and actions should help to create liking and respect for him in the prospect's mind.

Question—salesperson should ask questions indirectly as autosuggestion to reconfirm the sales story has become effective. The question could also be to elicit information in the form of investigation question.

Progress signal—The salesperson should look out for signals from prospect in the form of comment or action to confirm that the salesperson has fully answered Prospect Viewpoint Questions adequately to keep things moving.

Good judgement—classifies mindset operation where the ways of doing and saying things is done by Multiple Analysis for producing maximum benefits.

Command—any command used directly or with other counters that effectively produce desired result from the prospect.

First benefit—is the first result produced when a Good Quality is put to use.

Major interest benefit—expresses a result that is one of the prospect's objective.

Favourable condition—is when the prospect's industry, company, group, or personal life from where he draws benefits or will benefit in future, and that is brought to his attention to prepare him to visualise that he has an opportunity to Benefit still further through the salesperson's Proposition. The favourable conditions also appeals to Pride elements and gives him still greater power to help him to see and appreciate his Opportunity.

Unfavourable conditions—any situation that creates losses for the prospect, for which the prospect, the salesperson or his company are Not responsible and which brought to his attention discretely would help him to see the Need for the Benefits of the salesperson's proposition.

Spar—salesperson can use Spar as a special action for Mood and Manner, Assurance, and question, to meet the Obstacles in a serene and considerate manner so that the Objector's mind is reopened to reason.

3.7 THE TWENTY-FIRST CENTURY CHALLENGE

With the multitudes of competitive companies, national, international and multinational in the fray, the salespersons are facing probably the greatest challenge ever encountered by any salesperson before. They are required to call on to the full, all their personal resources to meet the challenge. Some salespersons with years of experience have acquired a name for themselves in the market. Now they are required to compete with highly respected and internationally known brands by retaining the existing business and adding new channel members to cater to some hitherto virtually unknown markets.

The challenge is great and yet there are ways and means of countering it and coming out a winner. The salesperson with fortified skills, and coordinated advertising campaigns is amply confident of meeting the challenges.

Challenges always brings opportunities and by effectively meeting the new competitive environment, the salesperson can develop self-pride as the salespersons grow in stature in the eyes of the management, channel members and the customers. The main objectives of learning about the twenty-first century challenges are the following:

1. To empower the salespersons, to meet the challenges with new skills, as their job becomes more rewarding and satisfying with new ideas and methods for achieving profitable results that will give you pride.
2. To improve the confidence level of the channel members in the company, as the salespersons with skills and ability would help the channel members in solving difficult problems.
3. To help the salespersons in effectively meeting the competition and with success their stature and value in the eyes of the company

and the customers will increase. Salespersons should develop better personal resources for achieving the kind of sales and profits results that will enhance their prestige and importance in their company and with the channel members.

Analysing present knowledge plans the students should attempt to understand the following:

1. Describe what they consider the basic goals or objectives of a salesperson's job.
2. Describe the Critical Success Factors for any company from the customer's, channel member's and the company's viewpoint.
3. Describe the type of relationship they should have with the channel members in the present highly competitive age.
4. Pick up a well known product and list down all possible benefit that would accrue to the customer by its use.
5. Describe what is considered as important for fighting competition.

Understanding people and dealing with them effectively.

Given below is Sales Analysis Chart

As effective sellers the entire approach to sales has to be customer oriented to be of any use. Hence the first analysis is from the customer or the prospects viewpoint as follows:

1. Attention — do I like and respect the salesperson?
2. Interest — what can his proposition do for me?
3. Desire — can he support his claim?
4. Decision — is it the best thing to do now?
5. Sale or Action — I will buy or act.

Given below are the Emotion Movers that persuade the buyer into favourable action:

1. Mood and Manner
2. Personal Prestige
3. Good Turn
4. Contact
5. Assurance
6. Question
7. Command

Reason Movers

1. Benefit
2. Good Quality
3. Poor Quality (negative for competition)

4. Loss
5. Proposition
6. Prestige
7. Explanation
8. Story
9. Good Judgement

The sale calls face the following obstacles:

1. Habit
2. Fear
3. Price
4. Complaint
5. Detail
6. Lack of Information
7. Competition
8. Friendship Competition
9. Difficult Personality
10. Time
11. Release
12. Divided Release
13. Negative Mood and Manner
14. Poor Judgement

As is noticed there are favourable and unfavourable conditions when the salesperson has to use or perceive the following:

- Use test question
- Perceive Signal

Obstacles can be handled by using Spar or practice or solution efforts.

Benefit Mover

A benefit mover describes clearly good result that a prospect will get from putting to use a good quality

Material benefits examples:

1. Save thirty thousand rupees
2. Reduce switching costs by 10%
3. Bring in more customers at lunch time
4. Enable you to finish your work in half the time
5. Improve the strength of the foundation

Physical benefits examples:

1. Make you more comfortable

2. Save you that heavy lifting
3. Prevent foot, leg, back pain
4. You can work in a more upright position
5. Keep the dust out of your nose lungs

Mental benefits examples:

1. You get more satisfaction out of your work
2. It will take a load out of your mind
3. Dealing with the company will be pleasant
4. The children will be perfectly safe
5. It may please the big boss

The benefit movers are having certain powers and some limitations too as given below.

Powers

The benefit movers enable the salesperson to predict for his prospect listener, the **interesting** and **desirable** results of doing what he has proposed. It appeals to the listener's basic motive for taking action in favour of the company. It answers the Prospects Viewpoint Question, " What good will your plan do?" and therefore noblest salesperson to talk from the prospect's viewpoint and best interest.

Limitations

The benefit movers lacks the power to support itself. It cannot answer the Prospect Viewpoint Question, "Can you support your claim" and therefore, unsupported, cannot give the prospect reason to believe benefit predictions or claims.

Good Quality Mover

A good quality mover describes the inherent trait or characteristic of a proposition or a specific part that makes it possible to produce Benefits when put to use.

Good Quality in Products

- Fine workmanship
- Improved design
- Mounted on live rubber
- Top grain cowhide
- Spring steel coils
- Three ply construction

Good Quality in Service

- Our servicemen are well trained and experienced
- Company is sound in finance
- We have carefully planned direct mail campaign

- We take hourly meter readings
- We apply heat evenly
- Our methodology is well tested in the field
- It is the practical way

Good Quality in Persons

- Honest and steady
- Skilled and experienced
- Intelligent
- Alert and enterprising
- Good natured
- Full of common sense
- Tactful
- Physically strong

The Powers and Limitations of the Good Quality Mover are given below:

Powers

The good quality mover enables salesperson to tell his prospect what makes possible the beneficial results of using the product he is offering. It has power to support the benefit claim and get them believed.

Limitations

The Good Quality Mover lacks the power to create interest and desire since it cannot describe the basic reason for buying, which is to obtain the Benefit

Analysing a Talk for its Movers

The student need to identify the benefit or the good quality mover as the analysis is made.

Example 1:

A bank equipment salesperson sees in a bank that the bus carrying bank money was being bumped against the walls, scratching and marring the walls. He got an idea and he expressed himself as follows in his talk with the bank personnel:

Salesperson—you could easily protect your walls and decorations by placing a continuous rubber bumper at the bottom of each bus. That would eliminate the scratches and the mars the buses make and save a lot of repair and maintenance costs.

Prospect—what are the bumpers like?

The talk has started revolving around the salesperson's objective.

Example 2:

An engineer wants his prospect to appreciate the Benefits that can be gained by the use of a automatic oil pump.

Engineer—machine shutdowns will be reduced to a minimum because this positive gear oil pump will automatically keep every bearing coated with oil.

Example 3:

Salesperson—you always wanted to guard your workers health, I have just the practical way to protect their lungs. Got the time to hear about it?

Prospect—I will make time. What is it?

Benefits are possible because of the Good Qualities of the product.

Example 4:

The shirt will be comfortable and long wearing because it is carefully tailored using terry silk material. It stays fresh, resists soiling all day long.

Analysing Product for Sale Movers

Salesperson needs to understand the sequencing of his thought process as he builds the benefit, good quality movers story. The analysis studies different kinds of reasons, as given below:

Product—Chest of drawers-extension arms

Benefits	Good Quality
1. file drawer can be rolled in and out of the cabinet rapidly with least effort 2. saves operators energy 3. reduce errors due to fatigue 4. gets the desired correspondence quicker 5. time and expense saved	Sturdy, steel extension arms using giant size ball bearings

Analysis of a proposition having both product and service parts

	Benefits	Good Qualities
Market Analysis		
Copy writing	1. First benefit-make a study of problems for which advertising is required 2. Write the copy then perfect it 3. Create copy that will get read 4. Bring inquiries	5. Trained and skilled copy writers, directed by experience and able supervisors
Art work		
Printing		
Papers		

Analysing a faulty situation for correction- machine operation

The correct plan		The situation	
Benefits	**Right way**	**Wrong way**	**Losses**
4. Keeps wrists for touching the bar 5. Machine will space perfectly	3. By holding wrists in arched position	1. Machine operator wrists sag slightly at times	2. Cuffs and wrists touch space bars that causes machine to space at wrong time.

The Correction Talk

Salesperson—(in a pleasant manner) the easy way to make the machine space perfectly is by holding the wrists higher than usual that keeps cuffs and wrists from even the lightest touch of the space bar. You get perfect results

The 4 Column Situation and Correction Analysis

Wrong actions:

1. Kitchen utensils stored where they cause the cook to take extra steps, not justified
2. Lawn mowing done in a shaggy way
3. Child strews things in a room which; looks dirty

Select a situation and analyse using the Analysis Sequence

Write short talk on correction of the situation, using the presentation sequence stating only the benefits which the right way of doing things will provide.

The thinking sequence starts with the wrong way and related losses and next come the right way and the benefits.

However, the Presentation Sequence starts by presenting the Benefits of the Right Way. The salesperson can mention the Wrong and the Losses only after pointing out the Right Way Benefits.

POOR QUALITY AND LOSS MOVERS

Poor quality movers clearly but tactfully describe the inherent traits and characteristics of a proposition, a situation or alternate product and plans that make it probable that the it will produce looses when put to use. It is recommended for highlighting the competitive products.

Loss Mover clearly but tactfully describes an undesirable result of putting poor quality product to use.

Examples:

1. Steel corners of the truck carrying money will mar metal work and plaster walls that will cause considerable repair expense.
2. Engineers have found that reinforcement of steel bars less tan 0.25 inch thick are too light and will fail to support even a slight overload

3. Untested methods might prove unworkable
4. Men lacking in experience can cause roads accidents

Power and Limitations of Poor Quality and Loss Movers

Powers

Help listeners to make wise choice when used after the Benefit and Good Quality Movers.

Limitations

When used alone, they often sound threatening, one-sided and arouse opposition.

Conclusion

Benefit and good quality movers are compared with poor quality and loss movers to help prospect reach the right decision.

Salesperson—in cold climate kota stone will stand up well because its square edges will hold mortar better during summer when the snow would melt. Slate has slanting tin edges which often fail to hold mortar when snow is melting and the sun is hot. Kota stone is cheaper to remain and hold appearance longer, I would recommend it.

(Students should analyse the sentence by segregating the benefits, good quality, loss and bad quality)

The material salesperson should arrange the 4 column analysis of sale movers as given below:

Kota stone	Kota stone	Slate	Slate
Good qualities	Benefits	Poor quality	Losses
1. Kota stone has thick, strong slabs, with square edges	2. Will hold mortar well in freezing and melting weather. Retain looks and appearance for years and is cheaper to maintain	3. Slate has razor edge thin slanting edges	4. Mortar will split away from edges during melting season, requiring expensive repairs

Multiple Analysis of Products

The analysis covers the benefits and losses of different products, including competitive products as it helps in making a comparative study on the product having more benefits and less losses in comparison to the competitive product.

Kota Stone

Benefits	Qualities	Losses
Hold mortar well under cool conditions or hot weather. Retain good appearance for years at low upkeep cost. Save on extra labour cost in a few years	Large sawn slabs having square edges one inch thick	More labour required to handle and to set. Costs about Rs. 10,000 more in labour to install
Slate		
Provides delicate beauty in pattern and colour Easier and faster to handle and save about Rs. 10,000 on labour of installing	Has a variety of colours and scalloped edged shapes. Edges thin and sharp	Mortar splits away from edges during snow melting season, beauty is marred, repair expense estimate at Rs. 5000 annually over ten year period

Analysis can be made in such a manner that only the benefits are highlighted as the losses are listed down by underplaying them. This gives the salesperson better idea on how to manage prospect's questions on competitive product. The best course ultimately is to lay stress on his own product Good Qualities and benefits that accrue through its use rather than decry competition where the chances of going wrong with incorrect statements are present.

Multiple Analysis of a Situation

The salesperson should make an effort to find the true interests of competitors with most benefits and fewest losses will be found.

Galvanised Conduit

Benefits	Problem	Losses
1. Initial cost less to consumer, it will help the dealer procure the order and a quick sure profit will be made by the dealer	2. Can the galvanised conduit be sold for use where acid fumes are present	3. Acid will get through the conduit. Corrosion, stoppages will occur. Dealers reputation will be damaged

Benefits	Problem	Losses
1. Consumer will find it will stand acid for years. Will save more than its cost by avoiding a single breakdown 2. More profit for the dealer 3. Effort to sell the right product will get respect of the buyers	2. Will there be stress on the buyer to buy zinc conduit with sealed surface?	1. Purchase will cost 40% more 2. Buyer may place order on someone else as his opposition may increase

In order to understand the above stated analyses the following dialogue gives real life situations that will take the students as close to corporate world as possible.

Reasoning Process in a Multi-comparison Form

Salesperson—(approaches his dealer, greets him pleasantly, shows appreciation for a new vehicle the dealer has purchased. Takes care of routine business and says calmly)-I talked to my office and was told you and one of your contractors were working on a major wiringjob with the Singh Corporation (pauses, waits for reply).

Dealer (says sadly)—yes, Ramesh, you know, the contractor is and he tells me that a young assistant to the Works Manager is deaf to everything but low price.

Salesperson (slowly and thoughtfully)—I see, well, he can make sure, quick profit that way.

Dealer—I guess that the young fellow is really tough. He is trying for a shrewd bargain. Just a wise guy.

Salesperson—yes, I see, how much does the company need protection? How corrosive is the acid?

Dealer—plenty. That is what worries me.

Salesperson—I can see how you feel . But as a guess, how soon the corrosion might develop into power failures and production stoppages, if these stocks are used?

Dealer—well, it will take some time, may be months. But a price-chiseller usually gets what he pays for. And some contractors go for low bids and quote these stocks.

Salesperson—it is a tough situation. I see that. There is a big profit if zinc conduits are used for all of us. But what will happen if the stocks are used when wire failure starts? Will this young fellow convince his boss that the contractor and us are to be blaimed and we will get a black eye with the local business.

Dealer—it could hurt the contractor. But people ought to know that a dealer only fills a contractor's orders.

Salesperson—they should know that. Do you think it would put the contractor in right with the customers Works Manager if he went to him and helped him to see the years of protection he will get by using zinc conduits?

Dealer—well-may be. Making a big issue of protecting each days production might even make a big change in the young fellow's thinking and make it unnecessary to go up. But as you know these contractors often make low bids and do not fight for zinc conduits enough. But if he had your kind of backing he would feel strong. So how about going to the customer with him? I think I can fix a meeting just now.

Salesperson—it is a deal. I will try to make the young fellow or his boss see how much more good the zinc conduit will do. Make sure that the contractor understands that in or lose we insist on zinc conduits.

Dealer—right boss. -(picks the phone.)

Prospects Basic Needs and Desires

Most people have certain common basic needs and desires as given below:

Security–people need protection from loss of what they have, protection to health, income, skills, mental powers, their company assets that are connected to their security and survival and of others whose welfare they have at heart.

Progress—people want to improve their personal and their team or group conditions, want to learn more, to do things better, besides they want the following:

- To earn more
- To live better
- To give better things and opportunities to their families
- To do work that increases importance and responsibility
- To help their company so that in turn they get more opportunities

Respect—people want the respect of customers, peers, employees, bosses, families and neighbours.

Satisfaction and Enjoyment from Work and Life — people want a sense of achievement, peace of mind, happy associations, a sense of belonging, a feeling that their work is important and beneficial, besides they want the happiness of doing more than just for money.

Responsibilities and Objectives of the Prospects Job

Once the salesperson appreciates and understands the type of responsibilities the prospects have he would be in a better position to tailor-make his sales presentation. A few of the responsibilities and job objectives are given below as examples:

President	Production Manager	Materials Manager
Keep company financially sound for survival, security and development Long term planning Build skilled competent management team for profitable successful operation Build company's Brand Equity Encourage and guide morale building Human Relations Get along with others and be respected Get satisfaction and pleasure out of work	Keep production levels high, costs low enough to beat competition Constantly improve production facilities Constantly improve people skills, knowledge Improve health standards, reduce accident rate Maintain and improve human relations. Keep morale high and be respected Get along with others both vertically and horizontally, while getting the things right Get satisfaction and pleasure out of work	Keep company adequately supplied and able to operate efficiently Avoid wastage of company funds Constantly improve the knowledge, skills, performance and morale of department personnel. Keep company's prestige high with sellers and secure helpful ideas and coopertion from them Get along with company's other departments, hold respect of their people and get department's helpful service fully understood and used Get satisfaction and pleasure out of work

Given below is similar statement for the supervisors and the workers

Supervisor	Worker
Get along with management and the workers Get work done on schedule Help to maintain and improve quality Keep costs low enough to compete and serve customer's best interest Successfully interpret workers problems and attitudes to management Successfully interpret company problems and policies to workers Hold respect of workers and others in supervision and management Handle complaints effectively and diplomatically and avoid possible grievances Be successful in persuading others to accept and cooperate with proposed ideas, plans Get satisfaction, pleasure and reward out of work and life	Be respected as a person by management and fellow workers Feel that the work done is important to company and customer Steady work and good pay Good bosses Chance to get ahead Good working conditions Job satisfaction, peace of mind and happiness

Salespersons having learnt the value of customer analysis needs to fit the benefits to prospects job objectives as given below:

Example 1:

The salesperson is talking to a road building contractor whose company security often depends upon making a profit in closely bid jobs. Hence that becomes his job objective and a major interest area.

Salesperson (for Road Grader is talking to road contractor whom he knows well)—to help our road contractor customers make a profit, our company makes a constant study of problems. The study goes right back to our designers. Take a tough problem of making a profit on closely bid jibs. One thing done, to help cut costs, to equip the controls of our new road grader with an improved hydraulic dumper. It eases pressure surges and eliminates the shock of starting and stopping the cutting blade. An operator can now place the blade faster and make more accurate cuts and yet do 20% more work per hour.

Example 2:

The salesperson talks to the Supervisor of the above stated road contracting company. He has learnt that this prospect has had trouble in keeping good operators because of many road jobs.

Road Grader Salesperson—to help, keep good persons on the job when they are long way from home, our designers have equipped the controls of the new model with improved hydraulic dumper. It eases pressure surges and eliminates shocks of staring and stopping the blade. With LESS effort, the operator can place the blade faster, make more accurate cuts, and do 20 percent more work. The workmen love the machine and they actually stay on the job longer.

The talk continues....

Fit the Movers to Prospects Job Objectives

The table given below summarises the way it is done

Part	Benefits	Good Qualities
1. Damper	1. Eases pressure surges 2. Cutting blade starting, stopping shocks eliminated 3. Blade placement by operator faster 4. Cut more accurate 5. 20 percent more work with less effort 6. Cut operating costs 7. Make a profit on closely bid jobs	8. New model controls have an improved hydraulic damper

The Bridge of Understanding

The FIRST BENEFIT expresses the first helpful thing a Good Quality will do for ANY user.

A MAJOR INTEREST BENEFIT expresses a final result that is one of the prospect's objectives

Operating cost cut	Up to 20% more work with less effort	Keep the depth of cut more accurate	Operator can place blade faster	Shock of starting and stopping cutting eliminated	Eases pressure surges
Bridge of Understanding					
Major interest benefit				Good quality	
Make a profit on closely bid jobs		Road Grader		New model controls have an improved hydraulic damper	

THE MOOD AND MANNER MOVER

A person's frame of mind and manner of speaking and acting that help to create liking and respect, is a Mood and Manner Mover.

When a listener/prospect sees a salesperson exhibit such Mood and Manner as the following, his emotions are favourable influenced:

1. Consideration and respect
2. Business like intent
3. Friendliness
4. Enthusiasm
5. Confidence
6. Tactfulness
7. Emotional control
8. Patience

Besides the above, when a listener /prospect sees a salesperson exhibit such Moods and Manners as follows his emotions are favourably influenced:

1. Earnestness
2. Seriousness
3. Due concern
4. Sympathy
5. Thoughtfulness
6. Alertness
7. Self-respect
8. Resolution

The inviting appearance of a shop, displays, product, brochure, person on the counter, that create a favourable impression and helps to create liking and respect are also classified under Mood and Manner Movers.

NEGATIVE MOOD AND MANNER

On the other hand there are Negative Mood and Manner that work as Obstacles as given below:

When a salesperson shows the following to the prospect through looks and actions his(prospects) emotions are affected unfavourably:

1. Selfishness
2. Arrogance
3. Impatience
4. Slyness

5. Overconfidence
6. Brittle temper
7. Insincerity
8. Superiority
9. Dislike

When a prospect sees a salesperson whose looks and actions indicate the following, the prospect's emotions are affected unfavourably.

When the appearance of a shop, display, brochure is uninviting and creates an atmosphere that puts the prospect in a negative mood, the Negative Mood and Manner is active.

Is Negative Mood and Manner an Obstacle?

Do the Negative Moods and Manners, shown in these examples, place a negative influence over all that is said and therefore weaken or ruin their reasoning power?

Example 1:

Supervisor — do you want to stay out of trouble with the inspectors? If so, watch these edges better. You are getting careless.

Example 2:

Salesperson—listen, pack the Glass RIGHT HEREAFTER, that is the only way to save us from this kind of trouble.

EMOTION MOVES USED TO PRESENT REASON MOVERS

Example 1:

An ASSURANCE MOVER is any combination used to present other Movers with tactful directness, or that has power to calm or reassure the prospect.

The Question Mover

A question used by the salesperson to present other Movers indirectly is a SUGGESTION QUESTION.

A COMMAND MOVER is any command used by itself or in conjunction with some other Movers that effectively produce a desired action from the prospect.

A STORY MOVER is an account of an occurrence that indirectly informs the prospect of Reason Movers, Emotion Movers or both.

AN ASSURANCE MOVER, USED TO PRESENT BENEFIT IDEAS POSITIVELY

Example 1:

Machinery Salesperson — yes, Mr. Gupta, your men will have even more protection than they have now.

THE QUESTION MOVER, USED TO PRESENT BENEFITS RESPECTFULLY AND OPEN THE DOOR TO MORE POSITIVE TACTICS

Example 2:

Salesperson to experienced retailer — what would you think of this idea for getting faster turnover on storage cabinets? (shows window display plans)

Retailer Prospect—why do you have household items rather than office items in two of these cabinets?

Salesperson—I think it will catch the eye of many of the women who pass the shop and bring some of them in to buy cabinets or some other items

(TALK CONTINUES)

THE COMMAND MOVER, USED TO PRESENT REASON MOVERS

Example 3:

Salesperson (to retailer)—take the lower profit, faster turnover plan!

THE STORY MOVER, USED TO PRESENT REASON MOVERS INDIRECTLY

Example 4:

Salesperson—over in Kolkata last week I saw how Hindustan Motors is making their big reduction in rejects. First of all, they are practically eliminating paint fading by---.(story continues)

It is interesting to understand that conclusions that are made are the product of a person's own mind and they become the basis on which he plans and acts. See, how well you agree with the following:

1. The basic motive in taking any action is to Benefit. A prospect can become INTERESTED only when he sees Benefits available
2. A prospect is a person or group that can be Benefited to a desirable degree and who has the money or credit or is able to take the action proposed
3. Effective planning of a sale begins with the finding of Benefits that will be interest to EACH prospect, Benefits for himself and others whose interest he has at heart
4. The Benefit Mover has the power to create interest by answering the Prospect-Viewpoint question, "What GOOD will your plan do?"
5. The Benefit, Good Quality, Poor Quality and Loss Movers have power to develop interest into desire to take action since they answer the Prospect Viewpoint question, "Can you support your (Benefit) claim?"

Three forms in which the prospects reason, when they make it clear that their purpose is to Benefit are as given below:

1. The Benefit and Good Quality Form
2. The Comparison Form
3. The Conclusion Form

Any form of reasoning can be in Assurance style, Question style, Command or Story style, or in a mixture of these styles. The Assurance and Command styles are Direct, the Question and Story styles are Indirect.

Styles of presenting Reason Movers appeal mainly to the emotions and have power to open the listening mind to the reception of speaker's reasoning.

The Mood and Manner Mover is an essential part of all presentation styles. It is the Emotion Mover that goes to work first in creating "liking and respect" and in answering the Prospect-viewpoint question, "Do I like and respect you".

Tact is practiced by avoiding the expression of Negative Impulse Judgments.

The recognition of Forms of Reasoning and Styles of Presenting Reason Movers will provide a guide for practicing TO-THE-POINT reasoning of Reason Movers. Such practice provides a background to present ideas effectively without conscious effort.

It is not expected that facing his prospect the salesperson will pause and say to himself, "Now I will use the Conclusion Form and present my ideas in Assurance Style" anymore than he will pause and think, "Now I will use a noun, a verb and an adverb".

THE PERSONAL PRESTIGE MOVER

A Personal Prestige Mover clearly describes the good reputation or achievement of the salesperson's company, its personnel, its products,its services or customers, endorsers who lend prestige. It provides the prospect with evidence that Benefit claims can be believed.

Example 1:

Purchase Manager to the Purchase Committee—the most experienced and reliable person in the paper business is Raghav Gupta.

Example 2:

Prospect on phone—Mr. Mathur told me of the clerical time and expense you have saved him. I would be happy if you come over to see me.

The examples show that good reputation built previously is active. In the next example the speaker tries to build his Prestige.

Example 3:

Salesperson—during the two years I was at the factory, a problem in electronic controls crept up and we could solve it in no time.

Example 4:

Manager to worker— sure, I know this machine, Verma. I operated it for four years.

Personal Prestige can be built by action.

Example 5:

Salesperson dismantles part of the machine he is selling and then puts it together.

Limitation

The power of the Personal Prestige Mover gets weak if the listener gets the impression that the speaker is trying to brag or is talking mainly to build his own confidence.

The Appeal to Pride Mover

An Appeal to Pride Mover confirms the salesperson's respect for the prospect by stating the achievements of the prospect, his company or by asking for advice.

Example 1:

Salesperson to his dealer—as I came in I heard some persons saying some nice things about the excellent job done on your display windows. You are making quite a success with you, is it not?

Example 2:

Salesperson to another non competitive salesperson—we are working on the colour scheme of our carton. Since you have done pioneering job in this area we would welcome any advice you would kindly give.

Example 3:

Salesperson—our engineers thought that a reduction in maintenance costs would be one of the main things, an engineer of your special experience would demand.

Example 4:

Service Engineer—the engineers in our Head Office will understand how you feel. They know you have always been fair-minded; so I am sure I can have this corrected in a day or two.

Example 5:

Service Manager—our Delhi Manager wrote to me about how well you planned the increase in sales of your engines in the North India.

Example 6:

Salesperson—I really like the hardwood shop floors, they look nice and long lasting.

Misuse of Compliments

Example 1:

Salesperson—you have a really well appointed office. It looks great.

The prospect has heard such a remark often over the past six years and further, he knows his office is nice but nothing unusual. On the day of the compliment it was rather dirty.

Example 2:

Salesperson—you have made one of the best displays in the windows that I have seen. However, the way the special products are displayed really look shabby from the street.

If you soft paddle your criticism with a compliment the listener will always expect criticism whenever you offer a compliment.

Example 3:

Salesperson of Bank Equipment to Bank teller—you sure can count money fast.

Teller—I ought to, I have been doing it for twenty years.

A prospect may not get any pleasure or satisfaction from a compliment on a task he performs as routine. On the other hand, a compliment put in a Question Style like, "in counting these brand new notes how do you keep a few from sticking together?" can Appeal to Pride Power.

THE GOOD TURN MOVER

A Good Turn Mover is a favour or free service performed or offered by the salesperson that has the power to build liking and respect and that places the prospect under no obligation.

Example 1:

Salesperson—you can have my copy of the Planning Commission's Report on the Five year plan.

Example 2:

Salesperson to the prospect—your supplier is in Rampur, is it not. I am going there tomorrow on business. Suppose I drop in at the supplier's place and see if I speed up things a little.

Example 3:

Salesperson to prospect—I just heard you are planning to go to Jaipur next Monday. I too have plans of going there by car. You are most welcome to come with me and I will drop you in Jaipur wherever you want.

Example 4:

Salesperson for Retail prospect—I have time on hand, if you want I can count the stock just arrived for you.

Example 5:

An experienced engineer solved his prospect's problem unconnected to his own business. In this way he did a Good Turn and later, the prospect said to another person in his company, "that fellow really knows his business" (Personal Prestige is earned through doing a Good Turn.)

THE CONTACT MOVER

A Contact Mover is defined as classifying the business or personal friendship developed between a salesperson and a customer or they mention of common friends, hobbies, and other outside interest activities that help to establish common interests.

When a prospect likes and treats a salesperson with more consideration because he is impressed by his Mood and Manner a Contact has begun. When a prospect is favourably impressed on finding that the salesperson is having a common friend or a person he respects, a degree of Contact is formed. When a prospect and the salesperson love to talk about or practice the same hobby a Contact is active. The strongest type of Contact comes about when the customer appreciates the benefits that the salesperson has enabled him to enjoy.

Examples of Contact Mover in action

Example 1:

Salesperson—I am Ramesh from Colgate company. Your friend Mr Kapil suggested I drop in and introduce myself.

Prospect—oh yes, Kapil phoned me about you.

Example 2:

Salesperson—I may have a solution to your leaks problem. Can I call you tomorrow, I want half an hour of your time.

Prospect—how about nine thirty?

Common Uses of the Command, Question and Assurance Movers

The student must understand that the Command, Question and Assurance Movers are not used only to PRESENT Reason Movers. The following examples:

Example 1:

Command mover—command used for routine directions.

Salesperson to associate—look at the second paragraph son.

Example 2:

Command used to calm the customer

Salesperson on phone—do not worry it will do your job.

Mrs. Raj—it will do the cleaning easily.

Example 3:

Question Mover used to elicit needed information.

Salesperson—at your Rampur plant how many barrels of oil you use daily?

Example 4:

Assurance Mover used to calm,

Salesperson—I know how you feel. I understand, you can rely on the delivery date.

Assurance used to calm, help and PREPARE the prospect to listen to reason.

ASSURANCE MOVER used to instill trust and confidence and to help to PREPARE prospect to open his mind to reason.

Example 5:

Salesperson—there are four models Mr. Roy. All are built differently. The one that will do your work best is model 3 (follow with the Benefit Mover).

The first two Assurances used in the example have power to build confidence in the prospect and they therefore help to PREPARE him to open his mind to the reception of Benefit ideas.

The purpose of Emotion Movers is to place the listener in a mood that will open his psyche to reason. The effective use of Emotion Movers, which is so much part of effective personality, is made possible by Sales Analysis. Such analysis often enables a salesperson to make specific improvements in his use of Emotion Movers. The foundation of instinctive or conscious utilisation of such Movers is the conviction that the listener can be Benefited to a degree that will OUTWEIGH the cost.

Getting the Sales Talks Started

Example 1:

Salesperson—I am Ramesh of Shiv Papers and since I am new to the area I came in to introduce myself.

Prospect—glad you did. Have a chair.

Salesperson—thank you. For the past five years I have worked out of Jaipur. By the way before I left, Mr. Gopal said to say hello for him.

Prospect—Gopal? I saw him at the Mumbai convention last month. Good man.

Salesperson—yes that he is. During the past three years he has taught me a lot about producing low cost frozen food boxes.

Secretary—sorry for interrupting Mr. Verma is here to see you.

Prospect—all right. Ask him to come in.

Salesperson—rising- thanks for letting me call on you without appointment. I am glad to have met you.

Prospect—yes, call me up in a week or so. I want to hear about the low cost boxes experience.

Example 2:

Salesperson is making a repeat call on a customer who has benefited a lot from the salesperson's company in the past. Personal Prestige and Contact are therefore established, plus a reasonable degree of liking and respect. On his last call he created Interest in a plan he proposed, was stopped by a problem and now he starts in a friendly and pleasant manner.

Salesperson—how are you Mr. Verma?

Prospect—fine. Thanks. Have a seat. I will be right back. (leaves and comes back shortly)- been to movies lately?

Salesperson—have not had a chance. I was called back to the Head Office. And while I was there I think we found the solution to your colour draining problem.

Prospect—is that so?

Salesperson—(continues his story)

***Example 3* — INQUIRY**

Prospect—(enters the office and asks)- is your salesperson named Sinha in?

Salesperson (who is in)—how do you do sir?

Prospect—my name is P K Agarwal of the Planet Publishing House. I have seen your desk top publishing unit with BB and Company in working status. I thought I would come in and see the new model 55 you advertise.

Salesperson—good. Come with me Mr. Agarwal and I WILL SHOW you the model. It is in the demonstration room down the hall. (PAUSE) I appreciate your coming I to see us and I am glad I happened to be here too. (PAUSE)—Do you have a problem something like what they had at the BB?

Prospect—no, we send out about ten thousand notices per month and they are printed as you can see. Raja of BB Company thinks your process might save us considerable money and I want to find that out.

Salesperson—(decides that the sale has MOVED into Desire zone for him and as he demonstrates the model he will carry on using rupees savings as his Major-Interest Benefit.-says)- I think we will find that Mr. Raja is right.

Types of Calls and Objectives of the Calls

The COMPLETELY CREATIVE CALL exists when the prospect has no intention of buying and when MOTION has to be created from the start.

Various Objectives of the COMPLETELY CREATIVE CALL are given below:

1. To get acquainted, build Personal Prestige, make a Contact and secure essential information for future use.

2. To get permission to make a survey or a demonstration or to get the prospect to try or test a product.
3. To start and move the Sale to Interest, Desire or Decision.

Partly Created Sales

The Inquiry—when the prospect has been moved to Interest or Desire to buy by means of advertising, satisfied customers, articles in magazines, and make an INQUIRY, one type of Partly Created Sales exists.

Objectives in dealing with an inquiry—to build Liking and Respect for self, to find out how far the Sale has progressed, to pick the Sale up at whatever point it has reached and MOVE it forward as far as possible by use of Emotion and Reason Movers.

The Favourable-Attention Call—when on his first Call the Salesperson finds that his company or product or plan is already known and respected to the extent that favourable Attention is easily secured, or when someone has built Personal Prestige for him or when a user has created Interest for him.

The problem for the salesperson is to capitalise upon the help secured and to use Emotion and Reason Movers to develop the Sale further.

The Follow-up Call exists when the salesperson has gained ATTENTION on a previous call or created Interest and develop it into desire to buy.

The objective is to maintain favourable ATTENTION by means of Emotion Movers and to MOVE the Sale forward by use of Emotion and Reason Movers.

The Service Call exists when the purpose of the visit is to Give service or find out if service is needed or to clear up misunderstandings or errors.

The main purpose of these classifications of the types of calls is to make it clear that wherever progress has already been made, it is not necessary to start back from the beginning but to use Movers to take it from there and carry on from the progress point that exists.

THE PRESTIGE MOVERS

When the good reputation of a company, its personnel, product or service or its customers and endorsers provides the prospect with evidence that Benefit claim can be believed, the Prestige Mover is active.

Examples of Prestige Movers in Action

User Prestige

1. The Delhi plant of Smart ACs have been using the system forte past ten years
2. The Parliament house, the President's house and the PMs house have all been rennovated by our company

3. Jayant Enterprises have been using our accounting software for the last six years.

Company and Personnel Prestige

1. The new monitoring software is one of the greatest achievements of our Research Laboratories
2. Each one of our GMs have received national commendation for their efforts
3. Our company has been the pioneer in seamless tubing, a fact that makes us proud
4. We are responsible of at least 70 % of production of artificial rubber in the country
5. We are the largest and oldest company in the business and also the most respected one
6. We hold the record of 100% zero defect production.

Product or Service Prestige

1. More of these painting machines are employed in the automobile industry than any other
2. It was the first cooker in the market and has remained the market leader ever since
3. The TV manufacturers of the country have taken our standards as their norms
4. Yes, this road paying machine is used in every state of the country.

Prestige of Process, Plan, Idea, Policy

1. The plan has been recognised by the Government recognised Railway Reconstruction Authority
2. The formula has worked in managing the mines in Bihar
3. Our MD has approved the idea to merge the two production units.

Problems in the Use of the Prestige Mover

Example A

Systems salesperson (After introducing himself, and having been invited to have a chair, thanks the prospect and says easily)-

From your recent magazine article I learnt of your interest in reducing the cost of operating records as well as machines. Since a practical and economically operated system for inventory control record has been developed by our company I hope you would like to see it. I have come with an invitation for you to visit our factory to give you a demonstration. Could you give me about ten minutes now

Prospect—smiles, let us hear it.

Example B

Systems Salesperson (After introducing himself and having been invited to have a seat, thanks the prospect and says proudly)-

My company is the oldest and largest in the field. We serve the Brass Group of companies. As an example of the advantage there is, in dealing with us, here is the inventory control system we produce for that group.

THE STORY MOVER

A Story Mover is on account of an occurrence that indirectly informs the prospect of the Reason Movers, Emotion Movers or both.

Example 1:

A salesperson whose products are industrial motors had, three weeks before, been told by a customer that cutting operating costs was his major problem. Now he returns and on his Follow-up Call, is told by a secretary that the prospect is about to leave for a trip through one of the company plants. Here is how he uses Emotion and Benefit Movers to answer the first two Prospect-view questions and thereafter uses the STORY to provide Evidence that his claim can be believed.

Salesperson—how are you Mr. Singh.

Prospect—very good, thanks.

Salesperson—do you remember that last month you had told me cost cutting was a major problem.

Prospect—it still is. I am about to leave for the plant and that is one thing on my mind.

Salesperson–good. I think I have an idea that can save them about 20% on finishing bases.

Prospect—that so? What is it?

Salesperson—by using a 10 hp motor instead of a smaller one and by using carbide cutters a smooth finish can be made with ONE fast cut. The reason I am sure of this is that I have seen it done at the bengaluru plant of HMT. As they stated, chips fall like gravel, deep and smooth cuts are made and their cost reduction has come to more than 25%.

Prospect—but what about the chatter?

Salesperson—I am glad you thought of that. They control it by----(talk continues).

Example 2:

Salesperson—(to customer who has just taken delivery of 10 drums of transformer oil)— I dropped in to thank you for your lube oil order and to make sure you have received in tact. Your stores Manager tells me that he is planning to move it into the closed store area this afternoon which is a good news, this will ensure that the oil is protected from moisture and hold its dielectric strength. The reason I am concerned is that two years ago a customer in Mumbai insisted upon taking delivery of 50 drums of the same oil, while they did not have storage room for the same. When I checked it had not been stored yet but they promised to get it under cover. However, it stayed outside throughout the monsoon. When they wanted to use it they found that its dielectric strength was affected so much by the moisture that it had to be condemned and they lost the entire investment.

The stories are given in some detail to show the various Reason Movers they contain.

Examples of some stories that have been used

Story that contains Appeal to Pride, Personal Prestige, Contact Movers. Used to build Liking and Respect

Story that Presents Benefit and other Movers indirectly. Used to answer Prospect's Viewpoint questions

Story of a company achievement in developing products, services or plans that increased Benefits to users. Used to support Benefit claims

Stories telling endorsements won from doctors, scientists, associations used to support Benefit claims

Story that presents Poor Quality and Loss Movers indirectly, following the direct use of Benefit and Good Quality Movers.

Research

Some examples of the use of Prestige Movers to research the need of company's products.

Example 1:

Salesperson—I heard about your big increase in sales in Gujarat, your dealers must be full of praise of your products and their lasting quality.

Prospect—we are proud of our record there, and all through the area for that matter.

Salesperson—the reason I came today to see you was on the problem of increasing the lifer of your cutting tools.

Example 2:

Salesperson—the last time I had called on you I was told about how you started out small and built this big business empire. The most interesting thing was how you made all the rich people of the town your customers.

It made me think that with such a fine trade, you are in a special position to make a nice profit on high quality storage cabinets.

Favourable Condition

A Favourable Condition is a situation in a prospect's industry, company, group or personal life that he is already benefiting or will benefit and that, when brought to his attention helps prepare him to see he has an Opportunity to Benefit still further through the salesperson's proposition.

When the efforts of the Prospect or his company have created the Favourable Condition it has appeal to Pride elements and stilt greater power to help him see and appreciate his Opportunity.

Appeal to Pride on Favourable Conditions

Example 1:

Salesperson to Distributor—you have built a fine team of salespersons, Ram. You can trust them to solve problems for your prospects and customers on your regular line. Hence, it seems to me you are set to male some nice extra profit by taking on small motors----(talk continues)

Example 2:

Research Officer to Management—the survey shows that the area has grown steadily for the last twenty years. It gives indication of continuous growth. Its per capita income is above the country's average. Its farms are highly productive and its manufacture diversified. While details are ready to be given, the general view is that it is a safe, profitable location for a storage depot.

Example 3:

Salesperson— how large is the payroll estimated for your new plant?

Prospect—around Rs. 100 lacs

Salesperson—so much! Well you must be bringing some top mechanical engineers too?

Prospect—yes, several, in fact.

Salesperson—what an opportunity for a housing complex, like this for instance(shows some layouts of such complexes that his company has built in the past.

Unfavourable Conditions

An Unfavourable Condition is any situation creating losses for the prospect, for which the prospect, the salesperson or their companies are NOT RESPONSIBLE, and which brought to the attention of the prospect, tactfully will help him see his NEED for the Benefits of the salesperson's proposition.

Part of the talk illustrating use of Unfavourable Conditions

Sales Engineer—as long as the coal is loaded in open cars in monsoon time, it will be full of moisture. When this coal is pulverised it packs like putty and causes sparkles in the furnace, that quickly lowers the efficiency of the furnace.

The one way to solve the problem of getting full efficiency from such fuel is, of course, to have a pulverize equipped with a properly designed hot plate.

Salesperson now shows illustrations and tells how the hot plate in his product dries coal and makes it as efficient as coal from the mine in proper condition.

The Difference between Unfavourable Conditions and Poor Quality and Loss Movers

The usefulness of separating Poor Quality and Loss Movers from Unfavourable Conditions for the prospect is that it reminds that Unfavourable Condition idea can usually be mentioned BEFORE Benefits without arousing resentment while Poor Quality and Loss Movers are effective when used AFTER Benefit and Good Quality Movers.

Example 1: Use of Unfavourable Conditions

Salesperson—is the monsoon giving your bus drivers the same schedule —troubles I hear so much about?

Prospect—it sure is. We are having our troubles.

Salesperson—to solve the schedule problems our engineers are doing a lot of careful research on wheel bearing protection.

Last winter, for example BEST in Mumbai made tests which, their records show make it possible to practically eliminate bearing failures---(develops the story)

Example 2: Use of Poor Quality and Loss Mover

Salesperson—I know you are having a lot of wheel bearing failures, due to the grease you are using and---

Prospect—where did YOU get the idea we are having a LOT of failures?-(relations can get strained)

Unfavourable AND Favourable Conditions used to prepare Prospect to Appreciate his Need and Opportunity to Benefit.

Example 1:

Salesperson—(has built personal prestige and contact)- how is the new raise in shipping rates going to affect your Kerala market?

Prospect—well, the southern competition will have the advantage in price. That is the picture.

Salesperson—what about this idea? With the dealers, there, getting such good prices and demand for your product, could you HOLD up your sales and profits if I could get you a big supply of rare raw materials at old prices?

Prospect—how big a supply are you thinking of?

The Proposition Mover

The name of the company and its salesperson, the product, service or plan and the price, terms of business, delivery are classified as the Proposition Movers.

Example 1:

The Capital Cabinet Manufacturing Company will furnish two models cabinets at Rs. 35000 each FOR Delhi net. The payment terms are 30 days from despatch and shipment will be made within six weeks of receipt of the order.

Example 2:

These direct mail folders will cost Rs. 25 each for a minimum order of 10,000 numbers.

Example 3:

The Singh Corporation offers this Annual Maintenance Contract for your Air Conditioners.

Example 4:

I am Mitra from the Krone Crane company.

Forms of Closing the Sale

The Benefit Sum-up and Close (Assurance Form)

Salesperson—to sum up, Mr. Roy, this cable will give you complete protection from breakdown. Your workmen will be protected from accidents due to the cutting of the cover. You will always be glad, you chose it.

The Benefit Sum up and Close (Question Form)

Salesperson—now, are there any questions I can answer about protection from breakdowns, or protection from accidents or time saving? Would you want it all sent to this mining area?

The Split-Decision Form of Close

1. How would you want it to be sent, by truck or by train?
2. Which colour would you prefer, white or blue?
3. Would you prefer a May delivery better than June?

The Question Form of Close

1. What is your idea on your quantity requirement?
2. How soon would you want it installed?

The Assurance Form of Close

1. You will do well to take this office Mr. Gupta.
2. Ramesh, I will order fast if I were you.

The Command Form of Close

1. Order the purchase now, do not delay.
2. Do what is recommended Mr. Seth?

Combination Closes

1. Do that Ram. You will be glad you did.
2. You will need it for monsoon will you not? If so, order should be placed now.

The Explanation Mover

Works used to make clear the meaning of a technical term or details of an operation, are Explanation Movers. Demonstrations, photographs, blue prints, when use to make details clear are too known as Explanation Movers.

Example 1:

The system should work well for us. The schedule is well planned. In this area the metres are ready on Tuesday. The billing machine operators prepare the ills on Thursday and they are sent to the customers on Friday.

Example 2:

It will reduce the amount of power required because it works on sound gravity principle shown here.

Example 3:

Salesperson—(about a poisonous matter sold as powder) you will find the material safe to handle and easy to measure as it is compressed into uniform tablets, looking like mini moth balls.

Example 4:

Salesperson—you place the sheets of paper on the transfer surface like this---and pull the lever---

Example 5:

To get perfect results you place the paper sheets accurately on the transfer plate like this---. Next you pull down the lever like this, slowly and evenly.

Example 6:

This is the delicious pure custard, we advertised in India Today. Ease taste it

The usefulness of a technical equipment is made easy and clear by demonstration and trial run.

Progress Signals and the Progress Test Questions

Progress Signals are comments and actions of a prospect that indicate that Prospect Viewpoint Questions have been or are being answered adequately enough to keep them moving.

A question asked by the salesperson to test the progress being made in a talk is a Progress Test Question.

Example 1:

Salesperson—your workers will be fully protected from shock-accidents since the tough tellurium cover has been placed on the cable. It ill protect the men even if they hit it with a pick axe.

Prospect—will it not cut?

Salesperson—it not only does not cut that way, it stays whole even if one of your switch engines accidentally runs over it. Does it surprise you?

Prospect—well it is a welcome surprise.

Salesperson—over at the Mayurbhanj mines the workers have not only been protected from such accidents, but there has not been a production breakdown, due to cable cutting in two years.

Example 2:

Salesperson—how does that look to you Mr. Prospect?

Example 3:

Salesperson—have I made that clear to you Mr. Prospect?

Prospect—yes I understand.

Salesperson—(continues his talk)

Example 4:

Salesperson—would it be safe to say that the time of at least two workers could be saved?

Prospect—well, I would say so.

Salesperson—in that case the system would pay for itself in just one year as its total cost is—

Example 5:

Salesperson—(after covering certain Benefit and several important Good Quality Movers)- that is sound construction, is it not Mr. Jai?

Prospect—good. Well thought out.

Types of Progress Signals

1. Prospect listens carefully.
2. Prospect nods and says "very interesting".
3. Prospect says, "I understand". That is clear.
4. Prospect asks, "sounds good but I do not quite see how the oil can do that?" (wants more information on Good Quality)

Test Question Types

(Sometimes they can be combined with other Movers)

1. Is that clear Mr. Ghosh?
2. Did I make it clear why the noise gets reduced by anchoring the motor like this?
3. Is the saving desirable?
4. Are you happy with the safety part of the investment?

Timely Placement of the Test Question

Success of The Test Question depends on keeping it in line with the Prospect View-point, question being answered and by not asking the question that goes beyond the information given to the prospect.

Examples:

Salesperson—is there a problem of that type in your industry?

Salesperson selling financial deals regarding security features of an investment-that is the most important thing for you is it not?

Salesperson—have we offered a satisfactory solution to your quality improvement problem?

Prospect—yes I think you have.

Salesperson—good. The next problem then is, can operating costs be reduced to a decent level----(talks carry on)

Limitations of The Test Question

The listener cannot answer in a manner that indicates progress if the question relates to something on which he has not yet been educated.

The question that ties back into a difference of opinion in a way that is embarrassing to the prospect is a non use of the test. For example, " do you see how wrong you have been?"

Obstacle Descriptors

Habit

The Habit Obstacle is active when a person has been performed a task in a particular way for a long time and just by the force of habit would not like to change even if there is a much better way of performing the task. Such people become immune to change of ideas and create a strong resistance to the progress of sale.

Fear

The Fear Obstacle is operating when a person has a justified fear of impending problems, of risk and consequent loss that overtakes his rational thinking. It causes him to by-pass the opportunity and keep performing below his potential with the help of new ideas.

Price

The Price Obstacle is active when the prospect does not realise the Benefits offered would outweigh their money value.

Complaint

The Complaint Obstacle is active when the prospect shows his dissatisfaction through words or actions.

Detail

The Detail Obstacle is operating when the prospect is of the opinion that the proposed plan is not worth, the effort it will require to obtain and put it to use.

Lack of Information

The Lack of Information Obstacle is operating when the progress of sales gets hampered when the salesperson has not yet fully informed the prospect or he lacks the information. At times the prospect may not have the technical knowledge to understand the proposal. Prospect may not be able to get the full significance of the benefits that will be enjoyed. It can also happen if the salesperson's talk is unclear or confusing to the prospect.

Competition

The Competition Obstacle is active when the prospect compares the Benefits or Good Qualities of the plan with another competitive plan and believe the later offers better benefits than the proposed plan.

(At times competition can be in dissimilar things like microwave oven and washing machine)

Friendship

The Friendship-Competition Obstacle works when a competitive salesperson or his company personnel has the liking and respect of the prospect and when the prospect believes that competitive product would produce similar or even better benefits.

Difficult Personality

The Difficult Personality Obstacle is active when a prospect lacks emotional control when he allows a difference of opinion to deteriorate into a personal attack or when he bursts out in anger, in rudeness, in deceit or other uncalled for behaviour which retards the progress.

Time

The Time Obstacle is active when the prospect thinks that the product or the plan under consideration is not worth the time it will need or it is late for making any changes. On the positive side the Time Obstacle can be used to convey to the prospect that any delay in decision will endanger success.

Release

The Release Obstacle is operative when the prospect wants to be released from further consideration of the plan.

The Divided Release

The Divided Release Obstacle is active when the prospect sincerely or insincerely seeks to end the interview by saying that he will take up the matter with a person not present.

Poor Judgment

The Poor Judgment Obstacle is created by the salesperson's lack of consideration in looking at the ground realities, in separating the right ways of doing things from wrong, in planning the sales call, in deciding how to use the Benefit Story from the prospect's Viewpoint. At times the salesperson can show disregard for the prospects reactions as the talks progress. The worst happens when the salesperson loses control of his emotions and forgets his knowledge of human nature and the practical selling techniques of study, analysis, planning and experience.

Examples of Obstacles

Prospect—your proposal is likely to upset our work. We would not be interested.

Prospect—it is too much money. There is no point in talking about it.

Financer—if we have to choose between air compressor you offer and the new furniture; one thing is sure our budget cannot stand both.

Prospect—if you had called even a week ago we would have been glad to have you in on the deal.

Prospect—we would need to keep our office force working overtime for weeks to install such a system.

Prospect—frankly, we buy all our supplies from X Tone Company. Swami of that company is very well liked around here.

Prospect—how do you people expect to be believed with your kind of delivery performance?

The Spar

The Spar is a special use of Emotion Movers, frequently Mood and Manners, Assurance and Question, to meet Obstacles in a calming and considerate manner so the objector's mind is reopened to reason. Conditions are also used a Spar at times.

The Spar in action

Example 1:

Prospect—what are you trying to get away with. This new machine looks hard to operate to me.

Salesperson—it does? Well, I guess it would look that way to anybody. Yet you will be running it like feather, touch only as an expert, in just two hours. I mean it.

Prospect—right-that suits me!

Example 2:

Lady Prospect—do not try to talk me into that. My husband would become mad if I bought the sofa of that colour.

Salesperson—he would? Well I can understand that — would this colour please him?

Example 3:

Prospect—Ram, we have been using riveted joints in our castings for years and our customers have been perfectly satisfied.

Salesperson—that is right Sir. It was the cost cutting angle I have been thinking of---(continues)

Note—The Spar may take just a second or two or it might be quite long.

How the Movers in the Spar have been expressed?

Assurance

1. I know how you feel-
2. I understand---
3. That is how it struck me at first---
4. I am glad you told me---

Question

1. Is that so?
2. It has?
3. You did?

Mood and Manner

1. Calmly
2. Sincerely
3. Earnestly
4. Politely
5. Sympathetically
6. Surprised

Meeting the Obstacles

Obstacle

Prospect—why we have to keep records for twenty years. Our work is quite satisfactory. Is it not?

Example 1: The SPAR

We know your work has been satisfactory. You have been doing great job. The idea now is to make your job more satisfactory to YOU, to lighten your rush hour burden. And with the modern visible record system, you will find it easy to keep posting up to the minute====

Example 2: The Dominating Method

Calm down. Listen to me. This is being done for your own good, to make it easier for you to keep your work and you better appreciate it.----

Check List for Situations

Does the company have a need for my Proposition? Can the money be secured? Have I got a Prospect?

Are things being done, used or planned by this company that are causing or will cause loss?

Are the laws, economic environment, operating conditions or acts of others causing Unfavourable Conditions that create a NEED for my product, service or plan?

Do Favourable Conditions exist that provide the Prospect with an opportunity to Benefit through my Proposition?

What Major Benefits can I use to answer the second Prospect-viewpoint question and create Interest?

How can I best expand and support my Major Benefit claims? Shall I rely on Benefit, Good Quality, Prestige and Story Movers or Poor Quality and Loss Movers essential for understanding and appreciation of the Benefits?

Of all the possible Obstacles which are the most likely to be active?

How can I use Major Benefits to avoid or weaken such Obstacles? Am I prepared to Spar effectively and make a good and sound Solution -Effort if Obstacles are voiced?

What company official should I see? What do I know about him? Is Personal Prestige or Contact active? How can I use Emotion Movers to build or maintain Liking and Respect? What Style shall I use to present my Major Benefit?

After studying the situation can I say that I have Faith in my plan? Do I FEEL that I can help the prospect reach worthwhile objectives and do I look forward to seeing him?

If satisfactory answers to all the above questions cannot be found before the sales call, tactful use of the Investigative Question will be needed during the call.

Prospects Situation

Started Day-Night Medical Shop

24 hour operation by medical shop in the heart of the City Centre?

Yes

Do you gain late and early hours business?

Yes

City laws permit 24 hour operation by medical shops.

Extra sales and profits

Earlier there was fear, lack of information and the force of habit inhibiting the prospect.

Extra profit outweighs extra expenses.

Sales talk outline

24 hours operation

Night service also friendly earnest and sincere

Business build plans to be worked out

Build friendship

Good operation, good staff, better service to customers

Good location

Extra sales, extra profits over extra expense

Night person hiring who can take care of details-send direct mail, post records in the computer, keep the shop clean.

Prospect—worth a trial, certainly!

Note: Benefit of the night person doing detailing work proved to be desirable to the prospect.

Sales Expense Budget—Marketing manager has the following expense categories in his department-

- ***Salaries***—these are normally standard and not subject to change except once a year when increments and promotions are announced.
- ***Travelling expense***—to keep a watch on travelling expense, the firm should plan structured tours of the salesmen wherever possible. Excegencies can be taken care of on ad-hoc basis.
- ***Research expense***—can be kept under control by keeping the research files updated by doing small surveys and also using secondary research when available.
- ***Communications***—telephone, fax, letters, judicious use of the facilities would help to reduce costs.
- ***Office rentals***—these are fixed expenses and not much, can be done unless some drastic steps are required like closing down some of the offices, when the firm may have decided to divest from some product.
- ***Stationery expense***—this is another hidden expense which if controlled can bring noticeable results.
- ***Goods transport/logistics/depots/firms own shops***—the chapter on logistics covers the expense control possible in the area.
- ***Commission to channel members***—the commission to channel members depends mostly on competitive factors and the strengths of the members. Dealers are for ever complaining of the bigger discount offered by the competition, which in fact could possibly be only a method of getting bigger discounts from the firm.

- ***Advertising and promotion***—use of advertising and promotion in these days of severe competition is absolutely essential for keeping the market share. To make these tools effective, pre-testing should be undertaken in all cases. At times, publicity, which is free, not paid for can help to build the firms image and sales much more than paid advertising as there is an aura of truth attached to publicity due to its editorial nature.

Yearly expense budget is made and reviewed on a quarterly basis to ensure that the people in the department are well within the allocated budget. Any deviations are also monitored, accounted for and justified. Corrective action where needed is taken.

Firm's profitability comes from the gross profit reduced by expenses. To increase profit, attempts are made to increase gross profit by increasing sales and by reducing expenses. Marketing manager must keep a close watch on the sales expenses; else even with increase in sale there would be lower profits. In most firms due to competition based profit squeeze, attempts are made on a continuous basis to keep expenses under control and budgeting is a method of achieving the same.

Sales Cost Control—as the costs of marketing comes from each of the salesman, the budget can be sub-divided into budget for each sales territory and the manager can keep proper control while approving the expense vouchers of the salesmen. Any deviation from the budget must have prior approval of the manager.

Reporting and Control System— in today's world of email and Internet, it is easy for the salesmen to post even daily reports to the manager. However, structured reporting helps as it becomes universal and not people specific. Besides travel itinerary, the salesman should send the following reports to the manager on a time bound basis to enable the manager to take corrective steps where needed and to provide the desired timely assistance to the salesman—

- Sales forecast and actual orders received, dispatches made on a customer wise product wise basis as per the suggested format given below:

Customer (Dealer) or Direct-customer________________ Period 2002-2003

Product	Sales objective	Orders received	Orders dispatched	Shortfall in orders/dispatches
PCs	250	210	205	40/45
Modems	120	120	110	0/10
Printers	60	35	30	25/30
UPS	100	80	60	20/40

Besides, a consolidated territory picture can be sent on the same base. Another report, which is important, is the age analysis of outstanding dues in each territory. And salesmen's plan on a time bound manner of liquidating the same, as can be seen from below-

The following format can be used:

Customer	Overdue amount	15 days old	30 days old	60 days old	120 days old	>120 days old
ABC Ltd.	3205000	200000	.1000000	1050000	500000	500000
XYZ Ltd.	2500000	2000000	500000	Nil	Nil	Nil

The form can be extended by one more column where the salesman can write the dates when the outstanding would be cleared.

Student's Discussion Points

1. What are purely the sales functions?
2. What are the methods employed for selecting and retaining salesmen?
3. How the tours should be planned to make them effective?
4. What are the methods, the salesmen should use in preparing their sales calls?
5. How should the marketing manager keep control of the salesmen's activities?

Business leaders have realized the importance of understanding the technological developments in the area of manufacturing technology and technology of product itself. Internationally they find opportunities emerging in a spectrum of nations that are ready to join the world market economy. The real effects of globalisation need to be seen in the context of opening of markets in hitherto closed countries, which were trying to safeguard the interests of their own industries. India was among these nations till 1991.

The other area that has emerged in recent years is the number and types of products that are available for sale. A partial list of the products is given below:

1. FMCG Products
2. Consumer durables
3. Industrial capital goods
4. Industrial consumables
5. Industrial raw materials and components
6. Services
7. Events
8. Ideas
9. Research outputs
10. Manpower
11. Property
12. Places

13. Information
14. Ideas
15. Organisations

Companies have found that unless they can build a meaningful relationship with their customers there is every possibility that the customers would go for competitive products. Companies have to build relationships not only with their user customers but also with the channel members, suppliers and even financers. These long-term relationships bind the company with these important groups of people for long-term loyalty on both sides.

Next companies need to learn the art and science of creating and managing demand of their products. Decisions on the marketing mix factors have assumed great importance with competition ever ready to look for loop holes in the companies planning process. Companies have to carefully formulate their product specifications, package design, pricing, channels of distribution, after sales service besides advertising and promotion. These need to be totally and directly in line with the customers' known and even unknown expectations. Product benefits for different customers have to be identified and refined to become close to the language spoken and understood by the selected customers. Companies have to carve out market segments for this purpose. Companies' plan marketing research for knowing the real needs of the customers, the way they buy the products, from mega marts, neighbourhood shops or from virtual electronic market place.

Companies have to find out on a continuous basis the changing environment of business and competition to remain proactive and ahead of competition. Michael Porter's five-force model is a good starting point for analysing competitive environment. Considering the competitive strength, companies can ill afford to remain oriented to production, as was the case in the first half of the last century. Today, market has to be main or the only focus for the companies while planning their marketing strategies. However, companies have to keep the interests of stakeholders in their decision-making and work towards a double bottom line that includes the welfare of stakeholders besides that of shareholders alone.

3.8 CUSTOMER VALUE

Customer buys products for the benefits he derives from the same. These benefits are the perceived values as per the customer's notions. The perceived value can be defined as the difference between the total customer assigned value and the total customer cost for buying the product. Sellers have to understand the perceived value by the customer and if it is low then the product is in the wrong market segment or is not being properly marketed. It is said that no body buys a product. People buy the satisfaction or the benefits the products provide to them. The seller may make tall claim about the value or product performance that will provide customer satisfaction or even customer delight. However, what really matters is the customer's belief regarding the product satisfaction levels with him. Providing customer satisfaction and customers delight has become the most important mission for the company and if the company can use it as its driving force it is bound to succeed despite tough competition.

Companies survive and thrive only if they make their customers loyal to them and add on to other customers, either from the non-buyers group or from among the customers presently buying from competition. The companies need to continuously innovate, research for new products for which the demand may be obvious or even dormant. Besides proper management of key areas as materials management with just in time inventory controls and training of the marketing personnel, both of the company and from the channel members would go a long way in optimized value chain management for the increased value addition for the customer. The supply line starts from suppliers of raw materials through the assembly process to the movement of finished goods to the customers' premises. Customers could be the channel members or the final users in case of B-to-B business. Companies with better supply chain management get sustainable competitive advantage, as they are able to deliver the products at the right time needed by the customers. Companies realize that it is much cheaper, (about 70 %) to retain customers than to get new customers. Financial benefits like loans, training in proper usage of the product, publicizing company's social assistance programmes like, free education for village children, adopting villages for overall development and even panting trees for providing green coverage in towns. These activities create goodwill for the company amongst the citizens, who are also the company's customers.

Product and service quality plays an important role in forming customers' attitudes in favour of the products. Consistency in quality, meeting the quality standards lay down by the government for the products (especially true for medicines and food products) and usage ease are the main factors considered by the customers regarding formation of attitudes towards the product. Initially, prospective customers try to get the opinion of their elders, peers and knowledgeable people about the product. Once they buy and use it their own experience forms their attitudes towards the product. TQM, Total Quality Management is therefore the essential ingredient in the success story as it is followed by TCM, Total Customer Management. Product quality is just one area of quality to be looked in to in TQM. Others are quality of service being provided to the customer, quality of knowledge about customers, and their behaviour, buying habits. Marketing research too requires top quality work for obtaining the correct information about the product demand, customers likes and dislikes and their buying patterns. For providing quality service, companies have to train their sales team along with the sales teams of the channel members.

3.9 SALESPERSON—THE STRATEGIST

Salespersons are known as the eyes and ears of the company. They are most reliable and timely source of information on market dynamics, business general and competitive environment. They are also the vital link the company has with its customers. They are the personal communicators to the customers, prospective customers and company's most effective PR persons.

Companies decide about the sales teams taking into account the sales objectives, the geographic area that needs to be covered, the distribution of sales territory amongst the team members and their compensation packets. Companies need sales persons who are committed and motivated to sell its products, who believe in its products, policies, and its culture and business philosophies. With increasing competitions, new players keep trying to attract the best salespersons. Companies must keep a close vigil on the loyalty factor of the sales team. For this reason alone, companies do well to keep them happy by providing them with adequate incentives, both monetary and non monetary like improved perks, paid holidays for good work done by them.

Sales team has the following tasks cut out for them:

1. Researching for customers, knowing their buying habits, likes and dislikes.
2. Planning sales calls on the customers and the prospects for effective results improving profitable sales.
3. Informing the customers about company's plans for product launches, pricing strategies and options.
4. Personal selling—this is the most important part both for Business-to Business sales and sales to the channel members.
5. Providing or organizing service to the customers for optimizing use of the products sold.
6. Maintaining relationships with the customers through non-sales contacts.
7. Gathering market information and communicating the same to the company.

Companies organize their sales teams in the following manner:

1. Dividing their sales area into territories that can be managed by a single sales person that are easy to cover, have enough business potential not to frustrate the sales person.
2. Recruiting the sales person considering their education, experience, personal background, ability and keenness to learn the companies' way of doing business and those who are happy with their initial package.

3. Training the sales persons into knowledge about company's products, sales policies, competition and the way they have to go about doing their business with on the job training (usually given by sending the recruit with experienced member of the team.), making them understand the communication plans for giving the correct benefit story to the customers about the products. Besides they need to be trained in relationship building both with external and internal customers and for being a good PR person for the company.
4. Monitoring and supervising the sales team for ensuring they achieve their targets of sales, expense budgets and profitability.
5. Motivating the sales persons through incentives, praise for jobs done well, for achieving targets.
6. Making proper evaluation of the efforts made by the sales persons individually and in teams to encourage team efforts.

Sales results come with a clear understanding of the sale persons about the customer's behaviour patterns, buying habits, buying motivations and buying periods. Besides, they should be fully knowledgeable in the art of salesmanship, the art of persuasion where the customer is lead through steps from his area of ignorance or even dislike of company's products to liking, and leading to purchase action. Later, they have to ensure proper usage of the products by the customers so that they derive the promised benefits from the products. This would lead to customer re-buy, retention and his loyalty towards the products and the firm. The decision steps used are given below:

Customer ignorant about the product	Inform about the most attractive benefit of the product to catch customer's attention
Customer becomes curious, still undecided	Give details of product specifications if required or just fresh lot of benefits
Customers says competitive product cheaper	Add benefits that overshadow the price
Customer says competitors offering free services	Counter by saying that while the product does not need any service, yet if required it would be given free of cost. Add testimonials from other satisfied customers
Customer says competitor product easily available	Offer to give most appropriate delivery time that would not add on to his inventory costs
Customer says he needs time to decide	Offer attractive some instant buy benefit
Customer places the order	Make sure of proper usage of the product by the customer, check out re-buy time

At times in the end when the customer is still dithering it is best to give him "either or option"-would like to insure the transportation or should we do it?" the moment he opts for one of the two, you can get his signatures on the dotted line of the purchase order.

Sales persons need to learn the art of negotiations that involves give and take. In such cases they must be fully aware of how much they can offer to the customer without losing out on the business and ending up in losses. They have to know the thin line between good business and a losing preposition. Sales persons should become genuine friends of their customer, never giving them wrong inputs, creating positive vibes for long term business relationship.

3.10 KNOWLEDGE BASE OF THE CUSTOMERS

Companies need to know the customers now than ever before, as with knowledge customers, companies have to provide them with a lot of information about the product, the company. Companies are facing non-price base competition where competitors are using credit extensions, giveaways, and financial help in the management of channels. Besides market economy and globalisation of the markets has clearly dictated that unless companies are fully knowledgeable about the customers and their needs, physical, psychological and sociological, companies could find themselves out of the market place, in the wilderness.

3.11 MARKETING INFORMATION SYSTEM

MIS provides the marketing team with reliable inputs regarding the market dynamics, demand trends, consumer behaviour and impact of competitive activities in the market. Companies could remain proactive as their MIS keeps their knowledge base updated always. MIS can be generated firstly from the company's own records like sales figures, age analysis of outstanding dues, new competition in the market, new customers gained and customers lost with reasons thereof. Besides marketing research fills in the information gaps and provides information on changing customer needs. Information on the market is gathered by the field sales force and can be termed as market intelligence as it incorporates subtle deviations in competitors planning and attitudinal changes occurring in the customer groups. These changes can happen due to new product introduction having better technology, greater advertising force of the competition, competitive promotional plans and new distribution methods adopted by competition that suit the customers better. Companies can update their MIS regularly with the help of computer that would store and analyse the information as required by the company.

Marketing research is today an essential tool in the armoury of marketing team. In the first half of the last century, most marketing decisions were made on the company's past experience and the manager's gut feeling. In today's environment such decision can only cause disaster for the company. Companies can have the option of getting the research done from within the company's personnel or it can get it done from outside. Research is done on scientific lines with some well-defined methods, after understanding the cost versus benefit analysis. Companies are using the research quite frequently to obviate defective decision-making for lack of information. Data analysis tools are available today that remove the incorrect data stream and lets the marketing team take more accurate decisions based on the research. Both qualitative research and quantitative research are undertaken for specific objectives for which the research has been envisaged. Therefore, the first essential decision to be taken is defining the research objectives, which should be clearly worded with no ambiguity, giving both the time frame and finance allocation made towards the research. The company could be having a marketing problem like loss of market share or it may be looking for an opportunity like introduction of new product in the market or yet still it could be for making marketing plans. Initially the company can look at the secondary data that may be available as it would be invariably at a much lower cost than a full-scale primary research. Exploratory research, focus group, panel groups can be tried before statistical research is undertaken. Causal research that talks about the cause and effect can be taken up in areas like for finding out the relationship between sales increase and price reduction. Market opportunities, new product demand, and competitive strengths and demand growth patterns can be understood through the research. Sales forecasts, marketing expense planning, production, procurements and advertising expenditure can be decided on the basis of the research. Research can give the demand pattern of the total industry product plus demand for individual brands. Sales force estimates, research data, managers gut feeling can be supplemented with test marketing of the product in the desired market segment, besides advanced statistical techniques, mathematical models regression analysis would lead to accurate forecasting of demand.

3.12 MARKET CONSUMERS BEHAVIOUR PATTERNS

Companies have to carefully understand the reasons why consumers buy their products, competitive products and they have to get the answers to the following questions:

1. What products are bought in the selected market segment?
2. Why these are bought?
3. What price the consumers are ready to pay for the products?
4. When they buy the product normally or how often it is purchased?
5. Where do the consumers buy the product-the right channel for market segment?

6. How do the buy-the buying decision process, influence of the family, friends, peers, celebrities and experts?

The factors that influence individual buying behaviour are the cultural milieu in which the consumers are living. Besides the societal factors like the social status, financial standing, family size and ages of family members are important factors. Besides psychographics and psychological factors are important considerations that cannot be ignored. These provide the motivation levels for making purchases and help in the formation of attitude, and beliefs. Buying is a complex process, especially of expensive products, where the following pattern is likely to be followed, may be with some variations at times:

1. Usually there is a user who wants the product for his use.
2. This person could be the initiator of the demand or it could be someone else too. For example, a teenage son may want a motorcycle and yet his demand may be placed before the head of the family, the father by his mother or elder brother.
3. There are at times people who influence the buying decision who could be a neighbour with a motorcycle or it could be the grandfather who is afraid that the teenager would meet with an accident and hence should not beg given the bike.
4. There are people who decide about the purchase, the deciders.

Each of the above people would have individual personality traits and buying motivations and hence while dealing with them the seller must give the benefit picture of the product in such a way that it suits the listener.

3.13 BUYING DECISIONS

Buying decisions are taken through the route given below:

1. Firstly, the need is identified or a problem that needs to be solved is located
2. Next information is gathered regarding products that would satisfy the need and solve the problem
3. Then the information gathered is shifted and evaluated for finding out the best solution
4. This would lead to making the purchase
5. After the purchase is made and the product has been used the after purchase actions take place, like repurchase, abandoning the product or finding out a new buyer for the second hand product
6. The total product cost includes the cost of the search for solutions, analysis cost, product price, maintenance costs as the sale price of the used product is deducted from the initial cost to buy and use.

3.14 STRATEGIES FOR SERVICES MARKETING

With rapid growth of service industry, its leaders have accepted the importance of services marketing. Service a product, has a product associated with it, as products too have service attached to them. Restaurants sell food to eat and that is the product while service is the main part of the business. Service product is intangible and usually gets destroyed if not used. An empty airline seat can never be used again and the customer enjoys the service but they cannot take it away with them. A passenger cannot carry the plane seat with him.

The way the service is provided to the customers can provide the service provider with Sustainable Competitive Advantage. Most five star hotels have documented and standardized methods of serving tea and coffee, liquor and food. Even then the scientific approach has to be carefully blended with the art of providing service. The quality of service separates different service providers.

Service industry is the one that analyses the customer's value to it. The big spender guest in a five star hotel gets a lot of freebees like fruit basket in his room, free entry to the hotel gym while the poor spender gets the normal facilities only. However, there cannot be any difference in the courtesy offered to the two as the hotel realizes that today's small spender can become tomorrow's big spender. Airlines have the frequent fliers benefit schemes like offer of free tickets, seat upgrades.

Service industry has not only to offer services to the customers but also ensure that the employees get trained in providing proper service to the customers. Bad service, rude behaviour will certainly put off the customer who would never come again for the service to the provider. With the advance technological innovations like e-booking, smart cards room entry (instead of the regular keys), automatic temperature controllers, hotels still have to ensure that soft areas like personalized pleasant service is the norm rather than an exception in the hotel.

Service industry has to ensure high level of quality service, high brand equity and easy access to their business areas. Service gives them the competitive advantage and there can never be any compromise on the same. The industry must train the employees for better service productivity, to ensure that their customers leave lot of their chores to the employees to have free time for their business and pleasure. Hotels arrange for unpacking of suitcases laundry and business meetings. The five star hotel business centres take care of customers including their business conferences.

Product companies provide post purchase service like the car sellers. They have to have service during the sales to convince the customers into buying their products.

3.15 STRATEGIES FOR MARKETING

India is a country where majority population, almost 70% lives in villages. There are 627000 villages in the country spread across its length and the breadth. However, the village people are poorer than the city people as the village contributes less than 50% of the total country's income. However, now the situation is gradually changing for the better.

There are 25 official languages and some four hundred dialects spoken in the country. Most world religions have their adherents here.

In the first half of the twentieth century, people were using neem or babul tree's twig for cleaning their teeth. Today, they are using tooth powder or toothpaste. Instead of groundnuts the children are asking for chocolate candies. Face cream or lotions have replaced Besan as a face cleanser.

Appreciating the size of the market, major companies, including, Hindustan Lever, P&G have made special strategies for targeting markets. Business environment in India is given below:

Demographic—the population has been steadily increasing in the villages, making per capita land holdings ever so small, reducing their income in the same proportion. This has resulted in migration from villages to towns either on temporary basis during off seasons for agriculture or on a more permanent basis as people come to cities looking for employment.

Social—there are women in the agriculture fields, in panchayats, child marriages are still prevalent in certain parts of the country, like Rajasthan. In certain states villagers have taken to arms and crime due to lack of employment, perhaps. Education levels differ from state to state, as Kerala boasts of highest percentage of educated persons.

Cultural—villagers celebrate festivals with a lot of gusto, especially the harvest time, religious festivals, marriages and childbirths.

Political—the green revolution was the result of the government's policy of research on agriculture. Milk cooperatives came about for the milk farmers with the pioneering efforts of the Amul organization. The government has been providing subsidies on farm inputs, tax holidays for farm profits, purchase of farm produce on a minimum price fixed by the government and has given a lot of concessions on agro packaging and processing industry.

Legal—government has enacted law against child marriages and dowry. However, it would need a concerted effort from the village folk themselves before the evil can be eradicated.

Macroeconomics—a lot of effort has gone into setting up of banks, farm insurance schemes. electrification, roads have been given priority in the governments planning process. Cottage industries and handicrafts have been given the desire impetus by the government.

Technology—today most villages of the country have the radio coverage and the TV spread is increasing by the day. Next, telephones, Internet would become ubiquitous in the villages soon. Tractors, harvesters, seeders, pesticides, fertilizers, quality seeds, scientific guidance on farming by the agriculture research institutes is enabling the farmers to get better yield from their farms.

Global—WTO has clearly defined the methods of agriculture exports from India and the government is finding it hard to counter the extra subsidies given by the affluent nations that make their products more competitive. Our leadership is busy in countering it through diplomacy in the WTO. Some countries have patented some of Indian products, like Basmati rice, turmeric, as their own much to the country's regret.

Products—most products required in cities are also needed in the markets with a few exceptions as given below:

1. FMCG products like cosmetics, food items like cooking oil, kerosene, and medicines
2. Consumer durables like refrigerators, stoves, motor cycles
3. Farm products like tractors, harvesters, seeders, seeds, fertilizers, pesticides, and diesel, water supply for household use including drinking purposes and for watering the farms
4. Services like, health clinics, water supply, electricity, eateries, inns
5. Housing.

Pricing in markets is tricky because the companies spend more on transporting the products as compared to transporting to the cities. However, the paying power in areas is much less. Companies can therefore plan to have low cost packaging with a bit of attractive glitter while keeping the product unchanged in most cases. The companies can work out the customers MTBP, Mean Time Between Purchase. They will find that the customer will stretch the purchase time much longer. This would be true for most FMCG products. Food items however would be needed as per household requirements.

❍❍❍

4

DISTRIBUTION OF GOODS

4.1 INTRODUCTION

Once the firm has completed Marketing Research and decided about the product/s they want to introduce in the market having selected the niche market, the firm needs to ensure that its customers and prospective customers are aware of the product and their usage, and the product is available to them at convenient shops. The first objective of communicating with customers is done through personal selling and advertising. The second is done through organizing proper distribution system. In this chapter we are discussing the distribution methods available for firms. The firms can choose the method best suited to their needs taking the product, its service requirements into account.

For the manufacturer of a product there are two basic distribution systems:

In the above method the manufacturer, sells by personal selling, through direct mail or from firm's own shops, (like Bata shops)

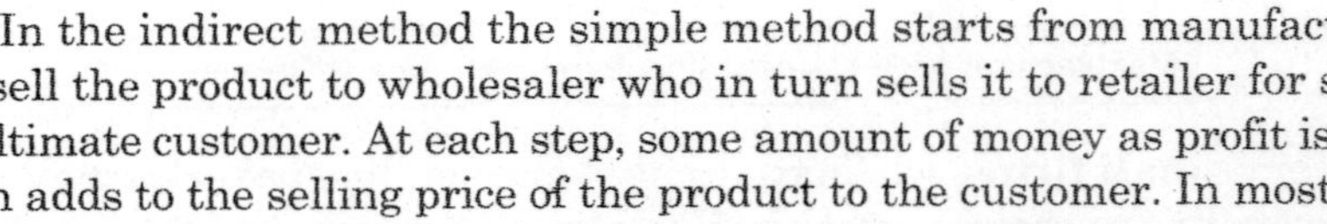

In the indirect method the simple method starts from manufacturers who sell the product to wholesaler who in turn sells it to retailer for sale to the ultimate customer. At each step, some amount of money as profit is given which adds to the selling price of the product to the customer. In most cases the manufacturer follows the set pattern of product distribution as per trade practices, or how the competitors are distributing their products. However, blindly following competition is not the answer, as competitors may be having different scales of production or any other basic difference with the firm. Innovations in distribution methods are taking place and firms should take advantage of the new methods.

Let us examine the two broad categories of products and their presently accepted distribution patterns.

Distribution patterns for consumer and industrial goods.

Industrial goods:

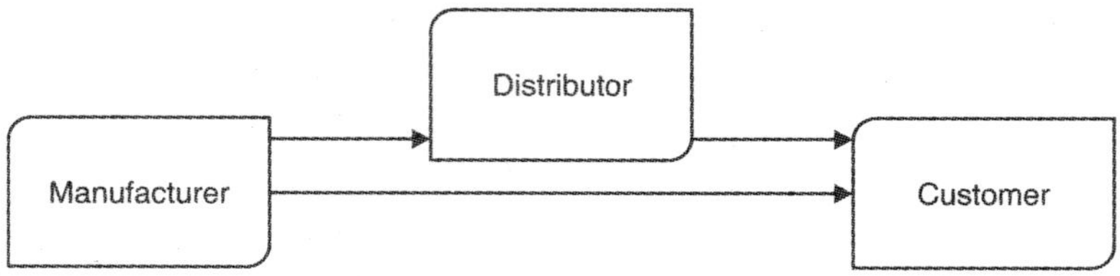

As can be seen, in industrial goods, the sale is made either directly to the customer or through a distributor. Capital goods sale is usually made directly to the customer, because of the following reasons:

- Technicalities have to be explained to the customer, which are best done by the manufacturer.
- Mostly large sums of money are involved and customer wants best price without middleman's commission.
- Installation and commissioning of the equipment is involved, best done by the manufacturer's engineers.
- After sales service is complicated.

In case of sale of Raw Materials and components the manufacturers sell through a distributor network the size of which is finalized taking the geographic area, which needs to be covered by the manufacturer.

4.2 CONSUMER GOODS

These are usually sold through the distribution channels as follows:

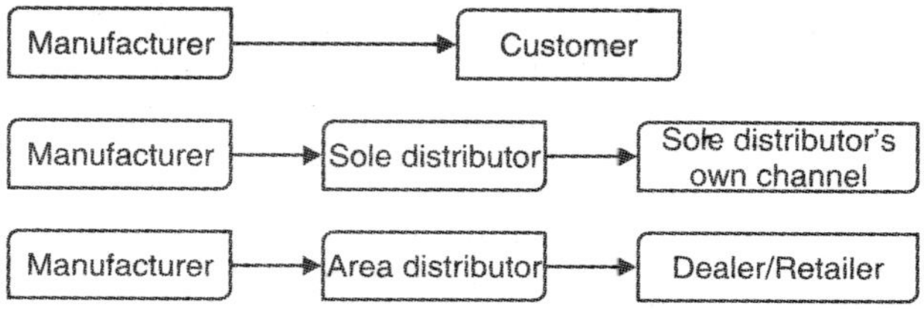

Very small firms, who have limited market, like bakeries may resort to direct selling to their customers. **Very large firms** have sole distributors with their own network of dealers and retailers. We will discuss the merits and demerits of each of the methods of distribution and some other methods as well.

Other distribution methods include the following:

- Own shops
- Mail order
- Web marketing
- Stockists
- Franchise outlets
- Catalogue sales
- Agency operations
- Consignment agents

Own shop—many manufacturers like Bata; Usha and Singer have their own i.e. company owned sales outlets (shops), these shops ensure that the products are available to the customer in good quantity, of right quality, at the right price. Besides, as the shops products of the firm only the control on sale can be more effective as compared to the sales being made through dealers and retailers who handle competitive products as well. The above mentioned firms realized the great assets they had in their own shops and as the firms had only a limited range of products, the shops, mostly in prime locations were not being fully utilized. These firms, therefore added complementary products and made their shops as sales outlets for complete range of products in their particular fields.

Franchise outlets—the manufacturers give legal rights to an independent business entity to run franchisers business (under some controls by franchiser, like quality control). The franchisers help the manufacturers to add to their business, have bigger geographic coverage and increase their market share. MacDonald's, Pizza Hut are two examples of manufacturers who have used franchise system effectively.

Mail order—some products like Readers Digest magazine are sold through Mail Order. Customers are requested to send their orders directly to the publishers, who send the product directly to the customers.

Catalogue sales—are a variant of mail order, as here the firms dealing with a number of products get colourful attractive catalogues made describing the products. These catalogues are then sold or distributed to a large number of prospective customers, who select products from the catalogue and place order on the firm. The firms have to ensure that the quality of the product sold is the same as mentioned in the catalogue; otherwise, the negative publicity with bad product sold will spoil the firm's business.

Web marketing—the spread of computers and Internet has opened the doors for marketing or selling on the Internet. Pick up any channel on the net and you will find a number of advertisements. The customers can place orders on the net itself and give their credit card number. The sellers will surely dispatch the product against the order. Since there are no expenses on shops, effective reduction in prices can be made. The only danger of these types of sales is that the customer does not get to see the product before they get the same.

Agency operation—agents are independent businessmen who help manufacturers in selling their products. The agents obtain orders from the customers, which they forward to the manufacturers. On the conclusion of the transaction, the agent gets Agency Commission for his efforts in getting the orders. Agents can be both for buying and selling products. They have long-term agreements with the manufacturers and they operate within the terms and conditions of the contract. Their task includes negotiating the sales contract with the buyers on behalf of the manufacturers for which they have the authority. They build long-term relationships with the buyers who benefit as they get consistently good products at uniform prices.

Stockists—manufacturers sometimes appoint stockists who are businessmen with storage space. The stockist's job is to keep stocks on behalf of the manufacturer and dispatch the same to distributors and retailers on receiving instructions from the manufacturer. For the use of their storage space and their efforts in making dispatches they get a commission from the manufacturers. Normally they are not involved in actual selling effort of the firm.

Consignment agents—these businessmen are required to keep stocks of manufacturers merchandise on their behalf and as and when they are able to sell the products they send the money received to the manufacturer. For their efforts they are paid a commission on sales. These types of agents are especially needed when a product is introduced in the market and the channel members are not sure of its saleability.

It can be seen that each type of distribution method has some advantages and some disadvantages. Depending on the product range, market segment, stage in its life cycle and capacity of manufacturer to produce, the channel is selected.

Unlike in the first half of the twentieth century, when the manufacturer as per his convenience decided the channel, now the channel selection depends mainly on market survey report, which tells the manufacturer, **how** the customer wants to buy the product. Main criteria can be summed up as follows:

- Customer reach for the channel
- Customer convenience of buying
- Service facility needed by the product and its availability with the channel
- Number of products available from one manufacturer for the channel

4.3 CUSTOMER REACH

Sales orientation of the first half of twentieth century was mainly on manufacture. Once the product is in the market it was sold. Competition was almost absent in most products. In some products there was total monopoly and the manufacturer could set his terms of sale. In majority of products however, there were a few manufacturers. In other words there was oligopoly and the manufacturers could join hands and control market prices. Later on in order to avoid the situation of cartel formation the Government of India set up Monopolies and Restrictive Trade Practices Commission (MRTPC).

Today in the beginning of the twenty-first century, manufacturers are facing severe competition in practically all the products and the manufacturer who can place his product within easy reach of the buyer definitely gains advantage over other competitors.

Taking this view Eureka Forbes has started personalized selling of their products, which include Consumer durables like Vacuum Cleaners, Water Purifiers. The sales are made by firm's salespersons visiting the homes and offices of prospective customers with sample of the product, when they can give live demonstration to convince the customers and obtain an order.

Many retailers have resorted to home delivery systems, including for consumer durables. The customer can buy a product by telephone order or through Internet purchase and the product is delivered to his home. Such purchases are paid for by either cash or through credit cards.

4.4 CUSTOMER CONVENIENCE BUYING

In every residential locality Convenience stores or retail outlets have come up. These shops keep stocks of a variety of products of daily needs, which the residents buy. As the shops keep competitive products they sell the products as per the following plan:

- Brand as per customers demand.
- Brand on the basis of sales commission they get from the firm. If the customer has no choice the shopkeeper will try to sell such a product where he gets maximum profit.
- In case the shop does not have the customer demanded brand it will try to convince the customer to buy the brand in stock.

No manufacturer can afford to avoid the retail shops, which cover the convenience criteria for the customers.

Sales with service—several consumer durable products require service to be provided to the product on either periodic basis like automobiles or once in a while basis like Air-conditioners. Retailers who can provide such service should sell all such products, which need regular service. Maruti car dealers are selected only on the condition that they can provide proper service to the sold cars. In fact, Maruti provides technical training to the engineers of their dealers. The dealers have to maintain stocks of spare parts and accessories, which enables them to provide timely proper service.

4.5 MULTIPLE PRODUCT MANUFACTURERS

When one manufacturer can supply a variety of products needed by one type of customers like, Hindustan Lever then they need to have distributors who can invest in inventories and prime location for their retail sales outlets.

We will discuss the value of Wholesalers in the distribution system. Manufacturers need retailers most, as they are the link between the manufacturer and the consumer. However, manufacturers find it difficult to sell to retailers direct, as they need small quantity of products only. Selling to numerous retailers would involve huge amount of billing action, several dispatches to a variety of locations needing enormous manpower. Wholesalers buy in bulk and hence selling to wholesalers reduces these activities. Bulk packing can be used for large consignments. Wholesalers also called distributors and perform the following functions for the manufacturer.

- Buy in bulk
- Making "small customer size" packages
- Buying variety of products and making matched sets as required by the customers, like soap and soap dish, tooth paste and tooth brush.
- Stocking products in large quantity ensuring that the dealer is never out of stock without having to invest in large inventory himself.
- Low cost transport to retailers can be provided as for small quantity they need not hire trucks. They can use tempos, three wheelers and hand trolleys.
- Provide information regarding competitive activities, new products in the market change in prices they can be virtual market surveyors for the firm.
- Provide credit, loans and leasing facility (either themselves or through a leasing agency) to the customers
- Share in advertising and promotion arranged by the firm.

As many firms are resorting to direct selling to the retail trade and sometimes to the customers, wholesalers may become obsolete in the future.

Wholesalers have been performing important role in the business of the manufacturers, most important being that of making bulk purchases. It is for this reason that the wholesalers prefer to sell products of only one manufacturer. They may take up sale of other manufacturer if there is no competition involved. Furthermore, wholesalers take up products from other manufacturers if they complement their main product either as an accessory or original component. The exclusivity of product sale is legally not appropriate under the MRTP Act. Most firms however keep the exclusivity clause in the agreement as unwritten.

In order to survive in the distribution race, Wholesalers/Distributors, have started to re-focus their strategies as under:

- Distributors/wholesalers divest themselves of small jobs and concentrate on the distribution as their main line of business. It provides the required focus to the task of distribution.
- Distributors/wholesalers take up product servicing as per standards laid by the manufacturers. They invest in service equipments, service consumables and stock of spares required for providing quality service to the customers.
- Distributors/wholesalers take up other customer oriented activities like providing leasing options to the customers, through their retailers.
- Distributors/wholesalers get their persons trained in servicing of product and in sales techniques. They impart this training to the sales and service people of retailers to enhance value addition to the products.
- Distributors/wholesalers help the manufacturers in meeting their sales targets.

4.6 RETAIL BUSINESS

has really come of age in the last decade of twentieth century. Retail shops have grown from being mere Storage Depots of the first half of twentieth century to the chain of super markets.

Historically, retailing started as sales by pushcart carrying products of daily use. The cart puller was also the salesman who vended the product in residential areas. In the morning the housewife found the bread and butter seller at her doorstep. These salesmen, on earnings saved hired or purchased shops in the same localities where they were selling on the carts. While they lost on mobility, they gained in larger product range, bigger clientele. Some shops became almost like morning clubs where friends would meet for making purchases and exchanging gossip and news. Despite the entry of super market chains, these shops have survived as they do provide a service to the local customers. In fact even handcarts have also remained as retail links and a large variety of products are still sold on the carts like vegetables.

At present also retail has not lost its importance, even one bit. In fact, there have been maximum innovations in the retail business as given below:

- **Super markets**—the one-stop shops. These shops are really multiple shops in one with large variety of products, sometimes complementary and sometimes totally dissimilar in nature and use. The common factor in all shops remains the type of customer who visits the shops. Now, the shoe shops sell sports wear, woollens, leather garments besides shoes. Gasoline stations have general merchandize shops from where patrons who come for filling their cars can purchase gift items, food products, and novelties to name a few products. Service centres have restaurants where the persons coming to get their car serviced can spend their time having a meal or snacks. Big departmental stores too keep a small eating areas and toilets for the shoppers. They have also added Children centres for the kids to have a good time while their parents do the shopping.
- Discount stores are coming up for several manufacturers. Products, which, have some small defect is sold at a discount at these shops. Manufacturers use these stores to fight competition. While heavy discounts can be offered on practically good products, no price war can be started on this basis.
- Boutiques have sprung up in most cities to cater to the elite of the town. These shops keep the latest fashion garments and other accessories. The products are high priced, as the customers are not price conscious, they are looking for something unique as status symbols.
- Super store chains have come up to provide same range of products, at the same prices and similar selling techniques. Normally, the customer has one such store near his house and he does not have to travel long distance to his super market for shopping. Marks and Spenser C&A in the UK are such chains. Now Delhi too has its own Marks and Spenser shop. With large volume business they offer competitive prices to the customers. The small shopkeeper with low volumes finds it difficult to compete with these giants. These Chain stores dictate their terms to manufacturers as they hold large volume business. They at times, get the manufacturers to supply the product in their own brand name, rather selling the product with manufacturer's brand.
- Shop-less shops — these sell products to customers through television shops, computer advertising and telephone marketing. Television has time slots during which products are shown and their use demonstrated. The customer is then requested to place his order on telephone for delivery to his for cash payment. Internet too is used to give product demonstration and orders are solicited through Internet only, with payment to be made via credit cards.

Telephone calls are used by tele-marketers, who give their sales pitch on telephone to carefully selected, likely customers. These calls are followed by visit of salesman to procure the order on the basis of telephone calls, which have, to an extent conveniences the customer into buying the products. With low overheads these sellers can offer low prices and one wonders if the days of Super markets are numbered.

- Retailers are now using the latest electronic products like computers for billing, inventory control, building customer database, and electronic anti-theft and surveillance devices. Bank retailing has gone to the extent of salesman less sales through Automatic Teller Machines the ubiquitous ATMs.
- Manufacturers' own shops — thus retail system has been tried by several manufacturers in India, like Usha, Bata and Singer. These shops have the advantage of providing the genuine products at company prices. Customers can get the entire range of products, the full variety. However, if the manufacturer's range of product is not large enough, the shop will not be a success as the customer's visits shops for a range of products where they get to see the full variety. A manufacturer of only toothpaste, handkerchief or boot polish cannot sustain to run a shop just for a single product. For this reason only, Usha, Bata and Singer have all started to sell a complete range of products even on buy-sell basis. Shops diversify their product range by adding similar products / products which go as accessories with their main products to take the synergic benefit of add on products.

Sole distributor—they work on volumes of business with low margins of profit, their market penetration is low as they depend on their retailers. With a large operational area they tend to lose grip on the market.

Area distributor—they cover certain geographic area and sell through dealers and retailers operating in their area. Usually area distributors work for one manufacturer only. At least they do not deal in competing products. Major problem in case of such distributors comes from area limits, as sales in other close by distributors area is affected by several distributors, which gives rise to conflict between the distributors.

Non-exclusive distributors—they deal in products of a number of manufacturers but they avoid having competing products.

Stockists — they keep manufacturer's stocks for giving to the dealers or retailers against authority from the manufactures. For this purpose they are paid a commission. Stockists help the manufacturers in faster supplies of products to retailers, as they are located near the markets, while manufacturing units could be quite far off.

Consignment sale stockists—they sell the product to the retailers after receiving the goods from the manufacturers without paying for the goods. Once they sell the goods they send the payment to the manufacturers.

To sum up the Distribution Method choices are as follows:

- Sole Distributor—Dealer———Retailer ____ A
- Sole Distributor————Retailer ________ B
- Stockist———————Retailer ________ C
- Consignment Agents——Retailer ________ D
- Agents———————Retailer ________ E
- Direct Mail ________________________ F
- Internet ___________________________ G
- Catalogue Sales _____________________ H
- Franchisee _________________________ I
- Own Shop __________________________ J

Needless to Add the Next Point of Sale is the Customer

We will now attempt to give weight-age to each of the above stated Distribution Methods on the following basis—

- Coverage of the designated area
- Concentration possible in the area
- Control of the manufacturer on the method
- Cost to the manufacturer

The following table gives some idea of these factors, although they may vary from product to product and area to area:

Distribution	Coverage	Concentration	Control	Cost
A	Wide	High	Low	High
B	Medium	Medium	Low	Medium
C	Medium	Low	Low	Medium
D	Medium	Medium	Medium	Medium
E	Wide	Low	Medium	Medium
F	Wide	Medium	Low	Low
G	Medium	Low	Low	Low
H	Low	High	Low	Low
I	Medium	Medium	Low	Low
J	Low	High	Top class	Medium

These values keep on changing and marketers have to understand the market dynamics before finalizing their distribution method.

In several product groups and markets, with the help of direct selling catalogue and Internet sales the middlemen as these intermediaries are called have been eliminated. They are supposed to be, by a section of society and business community considered to be only moneymaking bodies that do not perform any worthwhile task. The distribution chain adds to the costs of sale, which, ultimately the customer has to bear. As most middlemen do not perform any value addition function these could be reduced if not totally eliminated.

However, it must be understood that to remain in competitive market, the middlemen have learnt to provide value added services to the customers, like leasing, hire-purchase options, product servicing. Thus, they give the manufacturer chance of concentrating on production, product development and innovation, advertising and sales promotion.

It is therefore important for each manufacturer to weigh each of his concerns and then opt for a particular method of reaching his product to the people for whom they are meant and are produced in the first place, the customers.

Manufacturers like Eurekà Forbes have eliminated the middlemen altogether, while others with the similar product ranges are still using the time-tested methods. Personal selling like what is done by Eureka Forbes helps in building relationships, but it calls for huge investments in manpower, their training and area coverage's.

4.7 LEASING AND HIRE PURCHASE

Twenty-first century has seen great revolution in television and information technology in India. This has lead to much greater awareness of consumer products among the people. They are thinking of buying high cost products, which they may not be able to afford. Consumerism, keeping up with the neighbours is the trend today. Manufacturers and sellers both not only encourage the trend as it helps them sell more, they also facilitate the buyers by giving them deferred payment options. For financing purchase by customers, the sellers are taking the help of finance leasing firms. Now buyers can buy cars, houses and other luxuries without having ready cash for the purchase. They can get the money from the leasing firms, on interest. The advantages of lease purchase are given below:

- As no money is to be paid, or only a token amount is to be paid, the buyer tends to buy more; many times he buys things, which he really does not want.
- The buyer buys larger quantity than what he needs.
- Buyer can possess items much beyond his capacity to purchase and feel good.

- Buyer can make payments for the purchase as per his capacity to pay on a monthly basis.
- Products with low Brand awareness get sold.

The disadvantages of lease purchase are given below:

- Buyer buys products he does not want./Cannot afford
- Monthly payments can become a big dent in buyer's pocket
- Sellers may sell to a buyer who does not have the money to pay or may not have intentions of making the payments. In such a case the seller has to run after the buyer and he may have to resort to legal action to claim the amount, which is not good for business of the seller.

As in the west, especially in America leasing and hire purchase has become a norm, it is expected to take further roots in India also.

Firms who have selected sales through channels rather than by their own salesperson face the following situations:

1. Dealer/distributor should be selling only their products exclusively. In such an event the dealers are not allowed to sell competitive products. These dealers therefore expect the seller to be totally loyal to them and not sell their products through any other dealer or channel. The dealer expects the seller to remain competitive in the market and for this purpose he wants matching prices, discounts and other terms of business as compare to what the competitors are offering to their dealers. The seller has to remain vigilant in such situations as mostly the dealer tries to exaggerate the terms of competition for the better, which may not always be true. Seller needs to verify these statements from independent sources too.
2. Exclusive areas—dealers want the sellers to offer the products only to them in their designated area. The dealer also gets bound to sell the products in his area only. In case the seller finds the dealer is not selling as per his expectations, he has to either cancel the dealership as per the agreed terms or consider appointing other persons to sell in the same area. To avoid any conflict the dealership agreement should have a clause, which allows the seller to appoint more dealers.
3. Product bundling—many sellers try to sell their less selling products together with the fast moving one's. They sell the package deal or bundled products (popular name for computer software combinations). The dealers can object to such deals.

Monopolies and Restrictive Trade Practices Act, MRTP, as it is popularly known forbids the sellers to have such agreements and dealers can take recourse against any such practice by writing to MRTP. However, in practice, most such deals are done in full cooperation of the dealers and dealer agreements have only an unwritten clause for such activities.

We can summarize the activities of Distributors /Wholesalers as follows:

- Give large volume business to the manufacturers; operate through dealers and retailers to cover the geographic area assigned to them. Sell small number of items only. Sell to the second level of the distribution chain, the dealer or the retailer as also to bulk industrial buyers
- Purchase goods for resale from manufacturers in India or through imports.
- Some have their own retail outlets also.
- Have technical knowledge required to sell the product. Can provide product service to the customers.
- Make profits on large turnover even with low margins.

Similarly the activities of retailers can be summed up as given below:

- Sell a large variety of multi-brand products
- Sell in low volumes for each product as compared to the distributor of the product, who handles a large number of retailers.
- Sell to customers/consumers
- Purchase goods from wholesalers
- Location of retail shop, its façade, inner displays, window displays, salespersons and shop ambience are extremely important for the success of the shop.
- Profit margins for each product are higher than those of distributor
- Product mix, product shelf life are major considerations

With Internet marketing, telemarketing and tele-shopping networks, which sell through television, the established channel of distribution, may be threatened in the near future.

Case study -Competent Motors. Maruti car dealer and service provider.

Competent Motors are the authorized dealers (dealer term is in many businesses becomes synonymous with retailer). They are housed in a sprawling area close to the east Delhi residential colonies. They stock all the different models of Maruti car and have a good display of the models. A shade card nears the models tells the customer the number of colours available in that model. Next, there is an in-house accessory shop from where the car buyers can have the accessories fitted of their choice. The sales department takes the order and money. On the delivery point, the technical persons are present to show to the customers all the salient features of the car and its working.

Just before delivering the car, the salespersons give the options of license plate numbers. These plates are already in stock and are fitted on to the car in no time at all. If the customer is looking for leasing option or car purchase finance, the salesperson will guide him to the people from finance firms who are stationed there.

Competent Motors Service Centre—the same building houses the service centre also. They provide three free services to new cars as per the schedule laid down by the manufacturer. Afterwards they provide services for which the customer has to pay. As technicians have been trained by the technology people of the car, Suzuki, and only genuine spare parts are used during servicing and repairs customers prefer to get their cars serviced there only.

Recreation facilities—in case a customer has brought the car for service or repair, the Competent people offer to have him dropped in their own vehicle within a reasonable distance. However, if the customer wishes to stay on and take the car after getting it serviced, he can sit in a Coffee shop and have snacks or, he can sit in the lounge where a library, an indoor sports area and a TV has been provided for customer's entertainment.

Task for the Students

Compare the facility provided by the Competent Motors with the services provided by car sellers of the first half of the twentieth century. Discuss the reasons for the changes you find. Can something more be done to further improve customer satisfaction/delight?

❍❍❍

5

PRODUCT DISTRIBUTION MANAGEMENT

5.1 PRODUCT DISTRIBUTION IN MARKETS TAKES THE FOLLOWING ROUTE

Introduction

Products are kept for sale at the grocers' shops, diesel/kerosene dealers, and tractor repair shops. Besides, companies sell through mobile vans that cover the villages mostly on the days of their weekly markets. These vans carry advertising materials, audiovisual equipments for showing movies besides company's advertisements and the products for sale, samples like shampoo sachets for test marketing of the products.

Product promotion in markets is done through the vans. Besides, radio has a wide coverage as it covers the entire country geographically, is used. Additionally, television reach has increased of late and with better electricity availability it as become a good option, more especially because of its universal appeal. Pamphlets, loudspeaker announcements during weekly markets, mostly on roaming rickshaws, banner on elephants and camels are used in many areas.

Complete knowledge of the customer's requirements, problems which need to be solved.

Level of technology involved in marketing the product. This would decide if a technical salesman should be making the call.

Product knowledge and the benefits it offers to the customer in terms of safety of operations, economy, ease of usage and storage.

Qualities of a successful salesman

Goals in sales management

Goal setting process in sales management

Analysing market demand and sales potential

Techniques of sales forecasting

Sales budget
Selling strategies
Sales territories
Sales quota

Sales Force Management

Organising sales force
Leading and motivating sales force
Training and compensating sales force
Sales contests
Evaluation and analysis
Introduction to distribution management
Distribution of Goods

The students would learn the basic retail systems and understand their value in the context of retail thrust coming at staggering speed in the world.

It can be said without fear of contradiction that retailing has come of age in India. Retail industry is considered one of the fastest growing industries in world. India is considered as one of the most attractive retail destinations from amongst 30 emerging markets. India's vast middle consumer class and its almost untapped retail needs are main attractions for global retail giants wanting to enter newer markets. India's total retail market is valued at Rs. 912 Crore which is expected to grow at a rate of 30 per cent over the next five years. At present Retail Industry contributes 14 per cent to the national Gross Domestic Product (GDP). It employs nearly 7 per cent of the total workforce which means 42 Million (4.2 Crore) people. Retail industry is definitely one with immence growth potential from the Indian economy viewpoint.

The retail industry is divided into organised and unorganised sectors. Indian organised sector accounts for just 2 per cent of the trade and employs just 500,000 people. Unorganised retailing refers to the traditional formats of low-cost retailing such as the local kirana shops, owner-manned general stores, paan shops, convenience stores, handcart and pavement vendors, and employs about 40 million people. This sector is highly fragmented, with about 110 lakh outlets in the country.

As per the market figures the organised sector is expected to grow from two percent of 2007 to ten percent by 2010. With the rise in consumer demand, high disposable incomes and increased awareness levels, the retail industry is undergoing a major transition. Various functional aspects of retailing industry are given below:

Retail Merchandising and Category Management

- Fashion and Apparel

- Food
- Jewellery
- Lifestyle accessories
- Entertainment
- Retail Selling and Customer Service Management
- Store Operations
- Visual Displays, Merchandising and Store Design
- Retail Marketing and Customer Management
- In house shop entertainment, advertising POP.

Some of the major players in the industry are:

- Usha shops
- Bata shops
- Shoppers Stop
- Westside stores
- Subhiksha
- Globus
- Planet M
- Titan
- Madura Garments
- Pantaloon's Big Bazaar and Food Bazaar
- RPG group's Giant and Food World, and Metro Cash and Carry

Besides a large number of international and national players are planning to start operations in the country, like K-Mart in collaboration with the Indian telecom giant the Bharti group.

The Indian population is witnessing major changes in its demographics. A large young working population with an average age of 24 years, nuclear families in urban areas, along with increasing working-women population and emerging opportunities in the services sector are going to be the key growth drivers of the organised retail sector in India. And these would need unprecedented number of persons trained in specialized skills to run these organizations as given below:

Strategic management—strategizing, targeting and positioning, marketing and site selection.

Merchandise management—Vendor selection, inventory management, pricing.

Store management—Layout, merchandising and display, customer relationship, and inventory management.

Management—Administration, Human resources, finance, marketing.

Retailing today has become a vertical industry and is not just restricted to malls, as most tend to believe today. This industry offers ample opportunity and has room for everyone starting from entry level to senior management level in its present growth scenario.

Retailing provides employment to the largest section of the population across most industrialised nations. It is an industry that promises a profitable road. The boom in the retail industry has brought with it many employment opportunities in this area. People with varied skills and talents are required in this fast emerging industry. A career in retailing is considered a challenging option with growth potential as can be seen from the following-

Sales and Sales-Related Jobs

The sales and sales-related retail career area includes positions like salesperson, cashier, store stock supervisor, and stock taker/receiver. These frontline positions bring retail's core business of serving the customer and generating sales. The obsession for working with a variety of people, flexibility in mindset, level-headedness, problem solving ability, and teamwork are critical for success in this area. These positions are typically entry points into retail careers. High-end commission-based sales areas like jewellry, appliances, are preferred sales jobs. Frontline sales experience is valued and many retailers promote from within.

Store Operations

Retail professionals in the store operations career area, oversee overall store operations and profits. They include Head of Store Operations, Regional Manager, and District Manager, and responsibilities in this area may include functions like loss prevention and human resources.

Store Management

The store manager and his team has responsibilities ranging from departmental to overall establishment. Managers at all levels supervise and assist sales and other employees. Additional responsibilities, depending upon store/company size and management level include opening and closing the store, staffing, administration, and financial functions. Promotions to management positions can be earned through experience, and the right qualifications like an MBA degree may afford direct entry to management.

Marketing/Advertising

Depending upon company size, marketing functions may be centralized in one department, divided into different departments (like advertising, sales promotion, art and visual merchandising, and public relations), or group in various combinations. Marketing also conducts marketing research functions like focus groups and statistical analysis of customer buying patterns to develop strategies and plans that guide marketing components like ads, websites, store signage.

Distribution, Logistics, Supply Chain Management

This retail career area oversees movement and storage of saleable products. Responsibilities include management and facilitation of distribution centres, logistics, traffic management, trucking and other transportation operations, and may include import/export shipping and related duties.

Merchandise Buying/Planning

These retail professionals select the merchandise to be sold in the stores by sourcing vendors. They facilitate order follow-up, inventory flow through and allocation of merchandise to stores, attending to issues like flow quantities and timing. Statistical development and analysis are increasingly woven into this retail career area, where team members also coordinate gross margin planning and analysis responsibilities, develop distribution plans for merchandise categories and subclasses, and balance stock unit ratios by store on the basis of average sales in a given time frame.

IT and E-Commerce

Information Technology careers are numerous and varied in the retail industry. From web design to servers and network systems management, inventory systems and they are growing in the retail industry.

Finance

Financial and accounting skills are more than a game in retail; they offer career opportunities. The finance retail career area includes all accounting and treasury functions like accounting for income, paying expenses, compiling and maintaining financial records, money management and cash flow control, banking, investment, credit control, payment of the government taxes and audit.

Loss Prevention and Security Management

The loss prevention career area is responsible for safeguarding company assets and may include risk management issues, like customer and employee safety. Members of loss prevention team work together to prevent merchandise loss due to shoplifting, employee theft, paperwork errors, and vendor fraud. Physical security of store and company buildings is also a part of Loss Prevention.

Human Resources

Recruiting and hiring employees and responsibilities such as training, designing training programmes, overseeing compensation and benefits, and planning for and ensuring legal compliance in hiring and employment practices.

Entrepreneurship

Many retail career areas and positions offer lots of opportunities to be entrepreneurial, the responsibility of business ownership, profit and loss accountability.

The following qualities are essentially required in retail trade:

1. People skills
2. Zeal
3. Communication skills
4. Team spirit

The industry is set for a boom with the entry of big industrial corporations and international retailers making their entry into this sector. The industry constantly requires good, motivated personnel. It also promises a complete, enriching working experience with profitable inputs.

Specialised Distributors and Participants

Companies like Amway and Oriflame have innovated distribution where a housewives and other interested persons can take their distributorship, with the proviso that they would enrol other persons as distributors. These distributors do not have retail outlets; they buy for themselves and for sale to their friends, acquaintances and others while as a chain they add on other distributors like themselves.

These distributors have gained acceptance in the market and yet when the distributor chain breaks sales comes to an end.

- Selecting distributors and other Channel Members
- Following need to be considered while appointing distribution channel members-
- Requirements of retail space, finance, manpower
- Previous experience in selling
- Aptitude and interest

The actual plan would be based on products being sold and the distributors appointed are required to have a legal agreement with the manufacturers. The agreement needs to cover the following:

- Products to be sold
- Commission to be paid, including per unit commission, target based, yearly bonus commission
- Area of operation
- Sales targets (optional, as it keeps changing with time, however, a minimum can be fixed)
- Channel Conflict

At times a distributor could transgress into other distributor's territory, when conflict starts. An easy way to avoid such conflicts is to build a clause in the distributor's agreement that such transgression would incur heavy penalties. In some cases, however, the transgressing distributor has to share the commission with the legal distributor for the area.

- Training of Distribution Salespersons Channel

There are two basic types of channel members-

- Exclusive
- Multi-brand

In both cases it is important that the manufacturers train their salespersons for selling their products, the plus points, USPs, pricing, promotion plans. A classical example is given below-

Suzuki Motors as partner of Maruti had organising training of their dealer's sales and service persons in Suzuki headquarters training centres in Japan, at least in the beginning till they opened training centres in India.

Product Plans

Markets need practically all the products needed by the urban markets. Besides they have the especial requirements as given below-

- Farm equipments, like tractors, harvesters, seeders, ploughs
- Fertilisers
- Insecticides/pesticides

Introduction—it is the ingenuity of human mind, which, from the beginning of the time has invented innumerable products for the benefit of mankind. Imagine a life without the invention of wheel. And later on came the horse carriages, trains, trams and cars. What about the phones, which led to cell phones, videophones television and satellite channels? However for every successful product there must have been dozens, which could not see the light of the day. But the creative genius is not afraid of failures; he just pushes ahead with new ideas, products and services. Each firm sells the products needed by the customers. Each product has a definite life of its own. It takes birth in the inventor's crucible; it is then engineered for manufacture, made and sold. As newer products enter the market the old ones have to give way to them. This can be seen from the product life cycle given below:

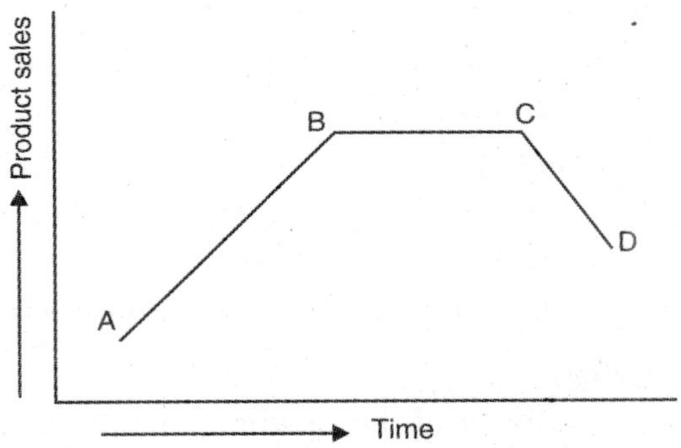

Fig.: Product life cycle

A detailed discussion on PLC is given elsewhere in the book. As the product is first introduced in the market the product sales volumes slowly increase from zero, as shown in segment A. Next comes growth stage where more buyers get to know about the product and they buy it and the business grows rapidly as shown in segment B. However, the growth gets reduced once there are no new customers and the product sales reach the maturity stage shown as C. Later on the product utility minimises and its sales start declining as shown as D.

The airline industry has found that they have basically two types of customers as given below:

1. **Business**—customers of this class want an air service which is, reliable, on schedule, with wide body aircrafts, easy to use airports with comfortable lounges, frequent flier programmes, telephone check-ins, variety of connections and in-flight entertainment. Possible upgrades from business class to first class
2. **Tourists**—look for low price travel, required schedules and several stopovers. For the sake of low price they do not mind night travels also. They look for package deals in which air tickets and hotel accommodations are all included.

Such details can only be found out by getting proper market research done.

Product Marketing Planning Process

Let us understand the formal process needed for planning marketing strategies in today's competitive age. Plans made should be a/short term b/ long term. Most firms make annual plans, which are divided into quarterly plans. To be entirely market proactive the plans should be kept flexible to enable firms to alter them to dovetail the changing market environment. The following steps are needed for making the plans:

- Analysis of External Environment
- Study of the Firms Internal Strengths and Weaknesses
- Idea Generation for Planning
- Brainstorming for Prioritizing the Ideas Generated
- Customer Behaviour Analysis
- Competitors Analysis
- Market Analysis
- Draft Annual and Short Term Plan
- Final Plans with Forecasting of Sales and Cash Flow

Customer's Analysis

We have discussed earlier why, how, where, when and how much the customer's buy, which can be ascertained with a degree of accuracy through market research. Let us take a simple **Customer Behaviour** pattern. It includes the following elements of internal information processing, guided by external information and stimuli.

- **Belief**—it is the customer's conviction and firm opinion of a product/brand
- **Perception**—it comes from a customer's product recognition as a desirable product based on his intuition and information gathered on sensory plane.
- **Attitude**—it is the customer's way of thinking about the product, his firm opinion about it.
- **Preference**—out of his belief, perception and attitude the customer makes his preference of one product over other products, and tries to buy it.

Thus we can define the Multi-attribute Decision Making process as, "based on concepts of Beliefs, Attitudes, Perceptions and Preferences" which is the notion that objects in a choice-set can lead to external behaviour. Each object in the set has a value on each attribute used to define the choice-set.

Let us take an example to illustrate the point. The purchase of a car in a family is a major event and decision-making process is multi-dimensional one. While film stars buy the car as a status symbol, middle class persons buy it as a means of transport only. Let us take four cars in the economy segment and plot their benefits to the customer. The figures given in the table 1.1 are only arbitrary and not conclusive.

Table1.1: Benefit story

Benefits	Esteem	Astra	Honda city
Comfort	7.5	8	8.5
Economy	4	5	6
Safety	3.8	4.5	5
Brand equity	4	7	6
Service facilities	9	6	5

The figures are based on a scale from 0-10

On a different plane another matrix can be made with benefits on one axis and decision making concepts for each car separately, before the final decision is taken as per table 1.2 given below follows:

Table 1.2 : Purchase decision matrix

Decision concepts/Benefits	Comfort	Economy	Safety	Brand equity
Beliefs				
Attitudes				
Perceptions				
Preferences				

The decision process, therefore, calls for a three-dimensions matrix, which would help the decision makers. This is done in steps as given below:

Definition of Retail:

Retail comes from the French word *retaillier* which means "cutting off, chip and divide" in terms of tailoring (1365). It first was recorded as a noun with the meaning of a "sale in small quantities" in 1433 (French).

Retailing is defined as to buy in larger quantities and sell on in smaller quantities. It is the sale of goods or merchandise, from a fixed location such as a department store or kiosk in small or individual lots for direct consumption by the customer/purchaser or end-user. It arranges goods in their finished state to be sold to the customers who are prepared to pay for the pleasure of eating, wearing or experiencing particular product.

Retailing may include auxiliary services, such as packing and delivery. Purchasers may be individuals or businesses.

The term retailing applies not only to the selling of tangible product like loaves of bread or pairs of shoes, but also to the selling intangible service products. Companies who provide meals, haircuts and aromatherapy sessions are all essentially retailers, as they sell to the final consumer, and yet customer do not take goods away from these retailers in a carrier bag. The consumption or use of the service product becomes the act of retailing.

Retailers buy goods in large quantities from manufacturers or importers, either directly or through a wholesaler, and then sells smaller quantities to the end-user.For example, a convenience store would buy tins of coke in units of two-dozen boxes, but sell as single tins. However, a retailer is not the only type of business entity to '**break bulk**'. A wholesaler also buys in larger quantities and sells on to their customers, mostly retailers, in smaller quantities. It is the type of customer, rather than the activity, that distinguishes a retailer from other distributive traders; a retailer sells to final consumers, unlike a wholesaler who sells on to a retailer or other business organization.

Baker (1998) defines a retailer as 'any establishment engaged in selling merchandise for personal or household consumption and rendering services incidental to the sale of such goods'.

There are, however, many businesses that carry out retailing activity that are not in themselves strictly classified as retailers; for example a factory may engage in retailing activity by selling 'seconds'-quality goods in the shop attached to its manufacturing premises. In UK a retailer is only classified as such for government reporting if the business gains over half of its income from selling to the final consumer.

Retail establishments are often called shops or stores. Retailers are at the end of the supply chain or the distribution channel. Manufacturers see the process of retailing as a part of their overall distribution strategy.

Retail trade or marketing: it is defined as "The sales made through a business location usually a store, in which the principal activity is the sale of merchandise and related services to the general public, for household or personal consumption".

An Introduction and Overview of the Retailing Business

The pricing technique used by most retailers is cost plus pricing. This involves adding a mark up amount or a percentage to the retailers' cost. Another technique is retail pricing, which involves charging the amount suggested by the manufacturer and usually printed on the product by the manufacturer as Maximum Retail Price-the MRP.

There are three major types of retailing as given below:

- First, is the **market**, a physical location where buyers and sellers converge. Usually this is located on town squares, sidewalks or designed streets and may involve the construction of temporary structures as market stalls.
- Second, is **shop or store trading** . Some shops use counter-service, where goods are out of reach of buyers and must be obtained from seller. This type of retail is common for small expensive items e.g. jewellery,and other controlled items like medicine and liquor. Self-service, where goods may be handled and examined prior to purchase, has become more common since the twentieth century.
- Third form of retail is **virtual retail,** where products are purchased via mail, telephone or online without having been examined physically but seen in a catalog, on television or on a website.

Building for retail have changed considerably over time. From market halls in the middle ages, which were essentially just covered market places to the departmental stores of nineteenth century, which were a street of several different shops, roofed over. One of the novelties of the departmental store was the introduction of fixed prices, making haggling unnecessary, and browsing more enjoyable. This is commonly considered the birth of consumerism. In cities, these were multistory buildings which pioneered the escalator.

In the 1920's the first supermarket opened in the United States, heralding in a new era of retail: self service. Around the same time the first shopping mall was constructed which incorporated elements from both the shop-rows and the departmental store. A mall consists of several departmental stores linked by arcades (many of whose shops are owned by the same firm under different names). All the stores rent their space from the mall owner. By mid-century, most of these were being developed as single enclosed, climate-controlled, projects in sub urban areas. The malls have had a considerable impact on the retail structure and urban development.

In addition to enclosed malls, there are also open malls which are 'outside" malls, and in Britain they are called retail parks. These are often connected to supermarkets stores. Also in high traffic areas, other businesses may lease space from the supermarket or store to sell their goods or services. A recent development is a very large shop called a superstore. These are sometimes located as stand-alone outlets, but more commonly are part of open mall or retail park.

Local shops may be known as brick or mortar stores in the United States. Many shops are part of a chain: a number of similar shops with the same name selling the same products in different locations. The shops may be owned by one company, or there may be a franchising company that has franchising agreements with the shop owners, including restaurant chains.

Some shops sell second hand goods. Often the public can also sell goods to such shops, sometimes called "pawn" shops. In other cases, especially in the case of a non profit shop, the public donates goods to the shop to be sold. In give-away shops goods can be taken for free.

There are also consignment shops, where a person can place an item in a store, and if it sells the person gives the shop owner a percentage of the sale price. The advantage of selling an item this way is that the established shop give the item exposure to more potential buyers.

The term retailer is also applied where a service provider services the need of a large number of individuals, such as with a telephone or electric power.

Retailer vs E-tailing

The word E tailing is derived from internet retailing or electronic retailing. E-tailing is emerging as an attractive alternative to the traditional brick-

and-mortar retailing. Chances are that they will co-exist profitably. Sometimes, a key question arises i.e. to retail or to e-tail?

The e-tail revolution: It all began a few years ago. Retailing as an attractive business was slowly emerging out of the shadows. Quite a few corporate houses began looking at retailing as one way to corporate salvation. Notable among them are: the R P Goenka group, the Tatas, the S Kumars, the Rajan Raheja group and the Ajay Piramal group. And many more are still in the process of finalising their forays into retailing. Even as loose ends of retailing plans are being tied up, e-tailing has begun catching the attention of many entrepreneurs. Suddenly, buyers started hearing e-tailing names such as Rediff.com, Jaldi.com, Fabmart.com, Tsnshop.com and Satyamonline.com. This could well be the beginning of an e-tail revolution.

The e-tail arena: How large is the retailing industry? Is e-tailing large enough to take on so many players? True, both retailing and e-tailing are still nascent and growing. One estimate by consultants KSA Technopak is that the organised retailing sector should be as large as Rs 5,000 crore and e-tailing in India should be just about Rs 12 crore. Says K Vaitheeswaran, vice president (marketing) of the Bangalore-based Fabmart: "But then the growth potential for both retailing and e-tailing is tremendous."

However, as one gets down to the nitty gritties of retailing and e-tailing, the differences in the way business is conducted in both the segments becomes clear.

Differences between the common retail model and the emerging e-tail model of online store retailers are as follows:

E tailing	Retailing
1. An e-tailer can go global.	1. Retailing is location driven.
2. Web-driven retailing, an e-tailer has no hassles of acquiring real estate.	2. In retailing, 50 per cent of the initial investment could go towards acquiring real estate.
3. The primary aim of every e-tailer is to attract a prospective customer to his e-tail site.	3. The primary aim of retailer is to maintain the continuity of distribution channel.
4. e-tailer has to spend considerable time, effort and money for a large ad spend. Adspends by dot.com companies are so huge that whatever savings achieved in the areas of real estate and inventory is more than offset.	4. Post-acquisition of real estate, a retailer has to spend considerable time, effort and money in setting up his shop, stocking inventory and creating display patterns.

Contd...

5. Customer retention is the toughest thing on the web and is certainly a costly affair.	5. A retailer expects strong customer loyalty,
6. Getting things are cheaper, easier and faster on the Net.	6. Getting things are cheaper and easier on the retaii outlet.
7. The Internet offers millions of products with no chances of an out of stock situation.	7. On the other hand, brick-and-mortar retailer who could offer you 10,000 items in his store. Chances are that he might be 10 per cent out of stock.
8. Easy and comfortably obtained info is another advantage that shopping on the Net offers. In the bargain, valuable time is lost. Simply put, shopping on the Internet for, say 15 minutes, could save a two hour trip to the mall. Consumers prefer to save this time so that they can devote more time for their professional and domestic priorties.	8. Traditional retailing stands out in stark contrast: the consumer searches frantically, runs up and down, grills a poorly trained store assistant who is unable to help him out. In the bargain, valuable time is lost.
9. The opportunities for personal attention available to the brick-and-mortar client are incomparably greater than those enjoyed by the Internet consumer.	9. The opportunities for personal attention available to the Internet consumer are incomparably smaller than those enjoyed by the brick-and-mortar client.
10. e-tailing names such as Rediff.com, Jaldi.com, Fabmart.com, Tsnshop.com and Satyamonline.com. This could well be the beginning of an e-tail revolution.	10. Started/initiated/begun by the R P Goenka group, the Tatas, the S Kumars, the Rajan Raheja group and the Ajay Piramal group, others are going to follow suit.

(1) A retailer is restricted to a particular location, retailing is location-driven. But, an e-tailer can go global. Being local in nature, a brick-and-mortar retailer has to identify a good location for his operations and wait for customers. A physical store caters only to a particular locality. On the other hand, an e-tailer has to virtually attract a customer to his website and offer him special services in order to go for a bigger and wider audience and still be in touch with individual preferences. In fact, location is no longer the key to success in e-tailing. While the target customer remains the same both in retailing and e-tailing, the mode of conducting business is changing dramatically.

(2) There is another distinct feature of e-tailing that is challenging. In retailing, as much as 50 per cent of the initial investment could go towards acquiring real estate. Post-acquisition of real estate, a retailer has to spend considerable time, effort and money in setting up his shop, stocking inventory and creating display patterns. Thanks to web-driven retailing, an e-tailer has no such hassles. But, there is a challenge before him: retaining a customer who has shopped through his site. He needs an eye catching website that brings the prospects to browse at the site.

(3) The primary aim of every e-tailer is to attract a prospective customer to his e-tail site. On the other hand, the primary aim of retailer is to maintain the continuity of distribution channel along with customer satisfaction.

(4) Attracting prospective customers calls for a large ad spend. e-tailer has to spend considerable time, effort and money for a large ad spend. Adspends by dot.com companies are so huge that whatever savings achieved in the areas of real estate and inventory is more than offset.

(5) After all that ad-spend, will the customer remain loyal to the e-tailing site? The Internet customer's buying behaviour is hard to predict and is different from the normal customer. Retaining him is not so simple. While a retailer can expect strong loyalty, such a loyalty on the Net is difficult to obtain. A customer may shift from the Internet if someone else offers him a better deal.

Jaldi.com will be using a mix of marketing tools such as public relations, advertising, promotions, direct marketing and Internet advertising to spread awareness among its target audience. Jaldi.com has gone a step ahead. Its offline promotions started with a successful consumer launch held at Priya PVR theatre in New Delhi where 3,600 free Phir Bhi Dil Hai Hindustani tickets were given to every customer who logged on and registered at the site Jaldi.com.

Summarising, customer retention is the toughest thing on the web. First of all, it is difficult to get a consumer come to your site. After he comes in, the task is to retain him and get him frequently. Once he is confident about you, he will use his credit card to make his purchases at your site. Hence retaining an e-tail customer is certainly a costly affair.

(6) If you offer some freebies, a customer may keep on coming to your site, with the expectation every time that there would be some freebies out there. The moment you stop freebies, you could simply lose the customer and managing e-tailing promotion through freebies could be a self defeating affair.

The first time a person shops on the Net is always a special occasion. If anyone has to try this new medium of shopping, there should be overwhelming reasons for doing so. The benefits must go beyond mere convenience. For one, the consumer will certainly be interested if he gets things cheaper on the net. The Net being a new medium, it has to convince people to use this new medium to buy. For convincing a customer to use The Internet one has to offer an incentive to buy on the Net. Otherwise, it would be very difficult to get a customer to shop. Therefore, easier and faster shopping are the reasons for shopping on the Net. On the other hand getting things cheaper and easier is possible on a retail outlet.

(7) One can go to a brick-and-mortar retailer who could offer you 10,000 items in his store. Chances are that he might be 10 per cent out of stock. On the other hand, the Internet offers millions of products with no chances of an out of stock situation.

(8) Easy and comfortably obtained info is another advantage that shopping on the Net offers. On the Internet, product information is just a few clicks away, all accessed in the comfort of a home. Traditional retailing stands out in stark contrast: the consumer searches frantically, runs up and down, grills a store assistant who may be unable to help him out. In the bargain, valuable time is lost. Simply put, shopping on the Internet for, say 15 minutes, could save a two hour trip to the mall. Consumers who prefer to save time so that they can devote more time for their professional and domestic priorities.

The Indian scenario is quite different from that of the West. For good reasons, Indians have always been great shoppers and enjoy shopping anywhere in the world. The lady would love to feel the silk of the dress physically rather than by viewing it on the internet. It would be only possible with a great deal of experience from the product purchase of the brand from normal stores that the buyers would venture to buy the same on the net. There are hurdles in India for any successful e-commerce project. Growth in e-commerce will come not from well-designed websites or web-marketing but from deeper penetration of the Internet. That is why a case has been made out for increasing broadband Internet connections which are faster than the dial-up connections, as can be seen below:

- One estimate is that India has a mere 20 lakh Internet users, mostly concentrated in the metros. Web analysts feel that in many areas of retailing and commerce, Internet is unlikely to get a sizable slice of the market, for several years to come. This is true, especially in businesses where margins are thin. Consider fast moving consumer goods, the FMCG sector. In the Indian FMCG business, margins are as low as 10 per cent. Hence, e-tailing in such areas might not catch on.

- Two, despite a higher Internet penetration, cities like Mumbai or New Delhi might not be haven for an e-tailer. For things like grocery, there is a shop at every nook and corner. All that an individual has to do is just make a phone call and the goods are delivered at his doorstep. Thrown in along with free home delivery is a month's credit. In case of perishables such as fruits and vegetables, the Indian buyers prefer them farm-fresh. While returning from work, they drop in at the vegetable market and complete their purchases.
- Three, cheap labour. Thanks to easy availability of domestics at an affordable wage bill, quite a few of the rich customers hire them for doing domestic chores which include shopping.
- Four, the usual Indian aversion to use credit cards. Thanks to low penetration of credit cards and the lack of popularity of debit cards, e-tailing might find it an uphill task to catch on. Also Elder citizens are averse to using even the computer. However, they are at ease while using the remote control of a television set. That brings up an interesting solution. Accessing the Internet through a television in the near future might be something that an individual should be offered if e-tailing is to grow faster.
- The last and the most important hurdle to the growth of the e-tailing industry is the efficient management of logistics. Here the role of a courier company is extremely important. Most portals offering e-commerce have tied up with courier companies. For instance, Jaldi.com has tied up with Gati for taking care of their delivery logistics.

There are other examples too. Blue Dart plans to enter the household shipment business in a big way to serve the needs of the online community in India. Looking at the coming e-commerce boom, Blue Dart is targeting a 80 per cent annual jump in its business, mostly from the shipment requirements of its online customers. For this purpose, Blue Dart has already invested Rs 40 crore to tune up its existing infrastructure and interface it with e-commerce potential.

On the technological front, Blue Dart is upgrading its intranet facility, linking 1,300 terminals with over 2,000 people at 70 locations to meet the e-commerce requirements. This means that e-shoppers in these locations can log on to Bluedart.com and ask for the shipment of ordered goods from these e-shops. Also, Blue Dart has aligned with leading portals and e-shops like Rediff.com and Fabmart.com to meet their distribution needs.

The most important question now is this: what kind of retailing model is going to deliver the goods in the India in the next few decades which is examined below:

- The most important cost advantage of e-tailing comes from elimination of intermediaries and economical distribution. For example, book e-tailing means dispensing with big shops replete with slow-moving stock. Consider the case of Amazon.Com, where the orders go straight to the wholesaler. That means the working capital costs are cut down drastically. Not just that, an e-tailer is paid before he pays his distributor and therefore needs lower working capital.
- However, one has to compare these gains against certain web-related costs. Running a website and servicing it to ensure that it is cent per cent reliable, is not easy. Logistics and distribution are of utmost importance and that is where many e-tailers are known to have gone wrong. While it is true that many e-tailers have been able to cut costs, they have lost large sums of money in the process of offering goods at low prices. A few of them who have made profits have ploughed them back for financing customer acquisition or retention.

All these do not mean an end to traditional retailing. E-tailing will have to co-exist with traditional retailing. For music and books, a whole new market will be created. This will increase the demand manifold. e-tailers will have to work in combination with traditional retailers. Even the known e-tailers in the business such as Amazon.com have realised this and are setting up distribution warehouses for the same.

As the combination of retailing and e-tailing set to deliver the goods, the trend of using the Internet as another service medium will gradually catch up. E-tailers like Jaldi.com have already set up kiosks in various cities which have been successful. Tsnshop.com makes use of its teleshopping network franchisees in various cities for selling its products. It helps in gaining customers fast, as individuals have the option of returning the goods purchased if they do not like it. They can just go across to the shop. This gives them a certain level of comfort and confidence. Such a comfort and confidence-level is a must for a successful e-tailing venture.

Summarising, what is being witnessed at the moment is certainly a tip of the iceberg. Such is the growth potential in the e-tailing industry that it is not possible to put a figure for the industry's size or growth. There are pluses and minuses in the case of retailing and e-tailing. With so many hurdles around for e-tailing, it would be long time before e-tailing really catches up as the trend has begun. The model which will work in such an Indian context is a peaceful and complementary co-existence of retailing and e-tailing.

The new technological capabilities, the internet, makes possible huge shrinking in the cost of access to customers that brings an additional threat to retailers in the form of disintermediation. Disintermediation is the direct selling of goods by manufacturers to consumers avoiding retailers. For example, Compaq sold its computers through retailers, whereas Dell computers grew rapidly by selling online. Established store-based retailers begin to doubt their future as more business go into direct online marketing. They fear, being disintermediated and losing out on retailing by the new e-tailers. While the prospect of disintermediation appears attractive, its implementation may be problematic for manufacturers. Majority of manufacturers are unwilling to sell online because of the nature of their product, and because of potential channel conflict. Disintermediation also requires heavy investment in the new channel that is unlikely to be profitable in the short term. The additional investment is not just in the internet/ electronic interface, but also requires infrastructural investments in the delivery of small orders. Such a strategy is risky as it assumes that a significant proportion of customers are prepared to switch channels, which may not be the case.

But disintermediation was only the half story. Although some middlemen lost their business, new middlemen sprang up to supply internet services to both businesses and consumers. Reintermediation took place on grand scale. As for the traditional 'brick-only" firms-Compaq, dragged their feet hoping that the assault of "pure click" firms would falter or disappear. Then they started their own online sales channel, becoming "brick and click" competitors. They had to do this carefully in order to retain the loyalty of retailers, brokers, and agents. The irony is two fold. First, many brick and click competitors became stronger contenders than the pure-click firms, since they had a larger pool of resources to work with and well-established brand names. And second, many formidable pure-click dot-coms started to falter as investors sensed a bubble, and began to disinvest, dropping the value of dot-com stocks, causing mass staff layoffs, and sending many-such as Pets.com, Mothernature.com, Boo.com, Garden.com, Eve.com- into bankruptcy. At the same time, many other pure-click dot-coms are surviving and even prospering in today's marketplace.

Development of the Retail Power

Earlier the producers of FMCG products, like Procter and Gamble, used to dominate their retailers, but the growing importance of mass distribution have transformed the power of retailers and now retailers tend to dominate the producers. In recent years, the number of products sold by grocery stores has grown faster than shelf life at the retail level. Retailers can now choose among an ever increasing number of products. Producers compete in order to obtain the shelf space for their products, and in the process confer a stronger bargaining power to retailers, who can threaten to take their products away from their shelves to obtain more profitable retail conditions. Shelf space has become the bargaining power and manufacturers are offering cash incentives for better and more prominent shelf space at the retail outlets and even rentals for decent shelf space for their products.

The reasons for the development of retail power are given below:

- Sales of most grocery items, drugs, and merchandising chains, have not been increasing at rapid rates. As the retailers need to grow, they must take sales at par with their competitors rather than waiting for overall demand to expand. This has created enormous pressure on retailers to perform, given that most chains tend to carry the same products. The type of competition tends to be price oriented. In other words, better prices coupled with prime locations, appealing stores, top-rate service have been the major routes to survival and success in this area. The chain retailers have increasingly begun to pressurize suppliers for price concessions and improved business terms like credit facility, increase in advertising expenditure. The power of producers is diminished by traditional retailers such as Wal-Mart, k-mart. Similarly, their power is being diminished by new retail entrants.
- In the competitive environment, the nature of supplier-retailer relationship in the grocery area have changed significantly. Retailers are concerned with improving their productivity. While it is almost impossible for them to raise prices, it is not possible to find ways to lower costs for increasing profitability. This can be achieved by achieving economies of scale, along with providing convenience of one stop shopping. They can build larger stores, increasing their fixed costs, creating higher break even points, forcing supermarkets and mass-merchandisers, discount stores to place even greater emphasis on generating larger sales volume. The resulting competition leads to consolidation, where stores tend to keep their dominant position by holding on to their tested strategies including penetrating pricing, advertising and promotion plans.
- There is increased pressure on employees of the retail companies. Earlier they focused on purchasing and maintaining balanced inventories. Now, they are profit centeres that are also responsible for capital management, service levels, turnover, retail margins and pricing, quality control, competitiveness and variety, operating costs, shelf space and position, and vendor selection and terms of purchase from them. In order to help the companies in making money, they look for suppliers to give them price discounts and merchandising support, and they become upset when these discounts and support are not forthcoming.
- Retailers have many new categories of products; they have to choose from them, what to stock on their shelves. The store sizes

have not increased significantly. Therefore, retailers are likely to choose products to stock on their shelves with a goal of making themselves profitable and viable and not the manufacturers. The manufacturer's bargaining position is weakened further because most new products do not succeed, by any reasonable definition of success. Procter and Gamble has responded to this challenge by decreasing the number of product offerings it sells to retailers. In addition, manufacturers have engaged in many new-product price and promotional allowances as a way of forcing their way onto retailer's shelves. These activities play into the hands of already powerful retailers.

- Information technology has spread throughout retailing to such an extent that virtually all of the major retailers can capture item-by-item data, via scanning devices, at their electronic point-of-sale terminals. The universal product code is used to help track the movement of product at retail and reduce both stockouts and supply cycle time.

The knowledge gained from market information has permitted retailers to calculate the Direct Product Profitability of individual items, track what moves and what does not move well in their stores, engage in forward investment buying, and leverage suppliers. The retailers use this data for their benefit and to coordinate the channel. For example, supermarket retailers can now tailor promotional offers to their loyalty card shoppers that link directly to their past buying behaviour, rather than needing to offer the same deal to all consumers. In one instance, retailers American Stores and Grand Union installed kiosks inside their store, accessible with a consumer's loyalty card, that distribute coupons related to shoppers prior purchases.

The Retail Marketing functions are given below:

- The primary focus is upon the major issues and strategies of retail management, including selection of merchandise, purchase, inventories, merchandising, product pricing and Point of Purchase advertising.
- Formulating retail strategy on sales promotion, advertising as a joint exercise along with the manufacturers based upon understanding of customer needs and buying motives.
- Evaluate and apply multi-attribute analysis given below, and other decision models to customers' brand choices, and choices of suppliers and merchandise.
- Organise basic concepts of economics, notably demand elasticity and diminishing marginal returns, to pricing, space allocation, service.

- Evaluate retail marketing performance through a range of quantitative and qualitative consumer research techniques, including focus groups, spot evaluation through questionnaire method.
- Analysis of Retail Markets—Segmentation of retail markets; consumer motives for selecting stores and centres; consumer images of retail companies and stores; target marketing and positioning.
- Retail Location and Planning—identification of optimum locations and the assessment of specific sites; catchment area analysis and models of retail location; issues and framework of town planning; the internationalisation of retail companies and store formats.
- Marketing Mix Strategies—retail pricing strategies, category management and buying, product range development and private labels, retail promotion and advertising, merchandising, space allocation and display, retail design and atmospherics, role and techniques of personal selling.
- Technology and Retailing—ways in which technology has impacted upon and helped to shape retail structure, for example, e-commerce, retail strategy like relationship management and retail operations.

Role of Strategic Planning in Retailing

Retailing is one of the key elements of a marketing strategy; it facilitates the market targeting process, making sure that a product reaches particular groups of consumers, the selected market segment. Retailing is important in a marketing strategy because it is concerned with matching the area in which a product is purchased to the benefits and characteristics of the product itself and its price as per customers orientation. Retailers provide a collection of service benefits to their customers such as being located in convenient places, editing product ranges according to shopping tasks, and selling goods in quantities that match personal consumption levels. Ensuring that this process runs smoothly presents a host of managerial challenges. Retailing is therefore a deceptively simple management process, yet fascinatingly complex in its detail, as the purchase motivation of buyers get more and more complex. The retailers need to have updated buyers behaviour pattern through a process of continuous monitoring and research. The strategic plans are created with the following areas of concern:

THE STRATEGIC RETAIL PLANNING PROCESS

1. Defining the business philosophy and mission.
2. Setting corporate objectives.
3. Situation analysis.
4. Identification and evaluation of strategic opportunities.
5. Development of marketing and positioning strategies.
6. Development of suitable retailing mix strategies.
7. Implementation and control.

1. Defining the Business Policy and Mission, and Corporate Objectives

The strategic planning process starts by identifying the firm's mission or purpose for its existence. A mission statement needs to identify the products and services to be offered and the customers to be served. It also needs to indicate how the resources and capabilities of the firm will be used to create customer satisfaction and how the firm intends to compete in its chosen markets. An example of a mission statement "Pfizer is a research based, global pharmaceutical company. We discover and develop innovative, value added products that improve quality of life of people around the world and help them enjoy longer, healthier and more productive lives. The company has three business segments: health care, animal health and consumer health care. Our products are available in more than 150 countries."

The mission also indicates the firm's philosophy for the way it intends to conduct its business. For instance, Panacea biotec's mission is "In support of life", this is supported by its goal of "To establish leadership areas through novel therapies and education", this reflects objective of "to be globally present as a healthcare company".

2. Situation Analysis

The purpose of situation analysis (also referred to as situation audit) is to determine where the organisation is at present and to forecast where it will be if existing strategies are pursued. The difference between the two is called the planning or strategic gap. The purpose of strategic management is to bridge this gap. Situational analysis can be divided into two broad components, namely external or environmental analysis and internal analysis. The purpose of external analysis is to identify opportunities and threats in the environment, and that of internal analysis to identify the key strengths and weaknesses of the organization.

The major components of external analysis are the macro environment and the task or operating environment. The macro environment consists of economic, political and legal, sociocultural and technological forces that affect retailers and over which they have very little control. The task environment, on the other hand, can be influenced directly by a retailer's own strategies and includes competitors, suppliers and customers. This can be best studied with the help of Michael Porters 5 Force Analysis.

The purpose of internal analysis or an internal audit is to assess the strategic capabilities of the retailer by examining the quality and quantity of resources available, how effectively they are used and the extent to which they are unique and difficult to imitate by competitors. Resources can be grouped into physical assets, human resources, financial resources, and intangible resources. Intangible resources include goodwill embodied in the retailer's own brands and the retailer's image.

Competitive Advantage and Competitive Strategies

For long term survival, retailers need to build sustainable competitive advantage (SCA) over their rivals in the market. Major methods of creating SCA include convenient locations, building customer loyalty, close relationships with suppliers, efficient logistics and supply-chain management, good information systems (including customer database management), exclusive merchandise (including own brands), buying economies of scale, superior customer service, and a knowledgeable and motivated sales force.

3. Identification and Evaluation of Strategic Opportunities

The retailer should be able to identify its key strengths and weaknesses and the major opportunities and threats that it faces by organising SWOT analysis - Strengths. Weaknesses, Opportunities and Threats. It is also sometimes referred as TOWS analysis emphasising that analysis of the external environment, threats and opportunities should take place before internal analysis, strengths and weaknesses.

After conducting the situation analysis the retailer needs to decide on the strategic direction for the organization as given below:

- Productivity strategies aim to improve earnings and increase the efficiency of current resource allocation through cost reductions, higher turnover and margins through an improved assortment of goods and higher prices.
- Strategies for improving efficiency include increasing inventory turnover by utilizing store space more effectively by better merchandising, reducing costs of labour, credit, logistics and other operating costs.
- Consolidation would require specific changes in the way the company operates. Recovering lost market share in the mature market is difficult. In mature markets retailers need to consolidate

their position by increasing emphasis on building customer loyalty through promotion programmes, improving service quality, increasing marketing activity of advertising, promotion, publicity and increasing emphasis on worker productivity improvements, through training programmes.

Evaluating Alternative Retailing Strategies

Having delineated the strategic options available, the retailer needs to decide on specific strategic action. This requires the evaluation of the strategies in terms of how they help to bridge the strategic gap between planned and actual profitability risk and the ability of the organization to undertake the particular strategy of penetrating or skimming prices. One useful method of doing this is to compare the attractiveness of the market opportunities with the competitive advantages of the retailer with the help of BCG matrix. The technique suggests that the highest amount of resources should be invested in opportunities where the retailer has the strongest competitive advantage. For instance, a retailer targeting a new segment would evaluate the attractiveness of market opportunity in terms of:

(1) Market size.
(2) Market growth rate.
(3) Degree of competition
(4) Profitability of the segment.
(5) Technology requirement —bar codes, computerised inventory and billing.
(6) Legal and regulatory issues.
(7) Human-resource requirements.
(8) Environmental issues.

This information must be compared with the retailer's strengths relative to that of competition on factors such as:

- Current market share.
- Merchandising skills.
- Buying strength.
- Supply-chain management and supplier relations.
- New product development.
- Own-label reputation.
- Financial resources.
- Sales force.
- Managerial competence.
- Fit with current retailer image in terms of breadth and depth of product lines, quality and reliability, customer service.

4. Development of Marketing and Positioning Strategies

Once the retailer has set objectives and analysed a number of opportunities it needs to decide on a specific direction for the organisation and the opportunities it wishes to take advantage of. For each of the opportunities chosen the retailer now needs to set specific objectives and allocate resources to achieve the objectives. In order to achieve the set objectives, marketing strategies have to be devised. These are normally developed for specific market segments rather than the market as a whole, as this makes more effective use of resources. After selecting the target markets a positioning strategy must be developed.

Retail Positioning

A positioning strategy is a plan of action for how the retailer will compete in the targeted markets and how it will differentiate itself from competitors in those markets. Retail positioning is the process of creating and maintaining a distinctive brand image of the retailer in the target customer's mind relative to its competitors. This emphasizes the fact that positioning is a relative concept and understanding consumers' perceptions is the key to effective positioning in the market. Positioning can be a deliberate attempt to differentiate from the rest of the market as Harrods have done, or an attempt to be as close as possible to the shopper's view of the attributes of an ideal retailer in a particular market segment.

Walters (1989) suggests that positioning should be either merchandise or service-led. He also suggested basis for positioning strategies to distinguish between symbolic and functional merchandise, and whether it attracts high or low margins. The reason is that people are motivated to buy the two categories and shop for them in different ways. Wortzel suggests three main positioning strategies, namely product differentiation, service and personality augmentation, and price leadership.

Product differentiation is achieved through unique or exclusive products or brands, own-branded products, and unusually broad or deep merchandise assortments.

Service and personality augmentation can be achieved in many different ways, including high levels of personal service, convenient locations, long opening hours, generous returns policy, home delivery.

Price leadership can be established through offering low or discounted pricing and good value or price promotions on key items.

Positioning is not a once-and-for-all decision. Because of changes in the market environment of consumers and the competitors, the positioning may need to be adjusted. Repositioning needs to be considered where there is a big discrepancy between consumers' perceptions and management perceptions. This is usually reflected in poor performance and declining market share. Repositioning can also be used to target a new set of customers.

5. The Retail Mix

The retail marketing and positioning strategy is put into effect by the retail mix - the set of controllable variables that the retailer can use to satisfy customers' needs and to influence their buying behaviour and compete effectively in the market. To implement a specific retailing strategy, managers must decide the best combination of retail-mix variables and coordinate the activities of the different elements of the mix such as given below:

- Merchandise assortment
- Location
- Price
- Visual merchandising
- Store atmosphere, ambience
- Customer service
- Advertising
- Promotions
- Personal selling

Walters (1989) suggests that positioning is the result of interaction between the four main areas of the retailing marketing mix; namely, trading style/format strategy, merchandise strategy, customer service, and customer communications strategy.

6. Implementation and Control

Without effective implementation, strategies are of not much use. Effective implementation requires that appropriate resources be allocated to required tasks, which requires budgeting in respect of specific elements of the retailing mix, personnel, shelf and floor space and merchandising. Effective implementation also requires scheduling and coordination of retailing activities. It needs the translation of retailing strategies into tactics. Functional strategies lead to the establishment of long- term objectives that must be focused into day-to-day operational decisions. For instance, when to advertise, what media to use, and the length of promotion campaigns are tactical decisions influenced by the competitive environment and the communication strategy.

The implementation of new retailing strategies inevitably requires changes in working methods and responsibilities which can lead to resistance from employees, and organisations need to develop strategies to reduce this resistance to a minimum and better still to totally convert them into believing in the new strategy as the management actively sells the new strategies to their employees. It is possible by the following method:

(1) Transparency in communication of changes being planned

(2) Equitable distribution of workload amongst the team members

(3) Training of the team for helping them to adjust to the changes planned

(4) Possibility of upward movement with the change for the dedicated few.

In order to assess how effectively strategies are being implemented and how far the strategic objectives are being achieved, control procedures need to be established. These control plans help to determine whether the objectives set are being achieved in the specified time periods. Such procedures allow unsatisfactory performance to be identified at an early stage, and remedial action or the reevaluation of retailing strategies and objectives to be instituted. Periodic reporting systems help the management in comparing the actual performance with set targets.

Emergent Strategy versus Planned Strategy

In practice, it is more than likely that the realized strategies are combinations of planned and action taken. However, the planning approach has the advantage that it suggests that retail mangers should be proactive in formulating retailing strategies rather than waiting for strategies to evolve. In the fast-moving retailing environment, proactive strategic management is indispensable for long-term survival. It calls for understanding of the retail business environment including area demographics, social and cultural milieu, economic standards, government regulations of shop and establishment act and competitive environment of existing competitors, bargaining power of vendors and buyers, threat of new entrants and substitute retailing like e-tailing, pavement shops and street hawkers.

Challenges and Opportunities in Retail Marketing

The retail movement in india has become the Sunrise area and the Retail Management or the Last Mile Management has the potential of emerging a clear winner. It offers tremendous opportunities for enterprenuers and the employees alike.

Retail transformation over the past decade has changed the definition of retail as manufacturers can no longer depend on sales taking place with inventory push alone. Retailing has gone beyond the realm of merchandising into Strategic Planning by creating a success story with the customer taking the centre stage as the retailers understand the aspirations,desires of the customers that help them in bonding lasting relationships with them. The knowledgeable customers of today expect much more than mere product when they make as purchase. They want more information about the usage, benefits and its life and sale value after they have finished with it. Retailers need to sell ideas, hopes and courtesy before they sell the product. Only then will retailers get repeat customers, loyal customers.

For manufacturers and service providers the emerging opportunities in urban markets are in capturing and delivering better value to the customers through retail. For instance, in Chennai CavinKare's LimeLite, Marico's Kaya Skin Clinic and Apollo Hospital's Apollo Pharmacies are examples where manufacturers and service providers combine their own manufactured products and services with those of others to generate value hitherto unknown. The last mile connect seems to be increasingly lively and experiential with the customer taking the centre stage.

Manufacturers and service providers face an exploding market, only marginally tapped due to difficulties in retailing. Innovative concepts and models are needed to survive and thrive in markets, because of the following reasons:

1. Poor infrastructure
2. Low income level of buyers with high Mean Time Between Purchases
3. Lack of retail shops
4. Lack of product knowledge.

Manufacturers and service providers will increasingly face a host of specialist retailers, who are characterised by use of modern management techniques, backed with seemingly unlimited financial resources. Organised retail appears inevitable. Retailing in India is currently estimated to be a US$ 200 billion industry, of which organised retailing makes up only 3 percent or US$ 6.4 billion. By 2010, organised retail is projected to reach US$ 23 billion. For retail industry in India, things have never looked better and brighter. Challenges to the manufacturers and service providers would abound when market power shifts to organised retail.

Organised retail too faces innumerable opportunities and challenges. The multitude of 'mom & pop' or the convenience stores are gearing up to face the organised retail by offering increased and personalized customer service. Organised retail faces challenges also in terms of product categories that it can profitably offer. Scale of organised retail demands the use of IT and sophisticated techniques to manage the supply chain and customers. For the organised retail, resources in these areas seem scarce. To conclude, every player in the arena, be it the manufacturer or service provider or the organised retailer, faces opportunities and challenges that can be met with flexible yet detailed strategic planning on issues like purchasing, merchandising and service to the customers.

For the last several years the local retailer has been at a major disadvantage due to the following reasons:

- Wide spread emergence of discount stores
- Internet as e-tailing has got the boost with high level proliferation of computers and the Internet

On the plus side a retailer is his own Boss.

All businesses start with a laudable intent, including retail business. It is therefore important to understand the business intents of retail entrepreneurs at this point, as different disciplines of retail have to interact with each other.

However given below are a few examples of these interactions:

- Finance with shares –company secretary
- Sales with accounts
- Personnel with finance
- Materials with logistics

No management discipline can operate as an island, on its own. The coordination of all the disciplines, as also of different stakeholders of the firm for generating continuous profitable results and growth firms, need to strategize their operations, else they are likely to go down in to oblivion in no time. This brings in the holistic planning in a firm covering the entire gamut of activities and thought process. Even TQM, which was considered applicable only in manufacturing, has become an all-pervasive tool, which affects the entire organization today. It is however unfortunate that in practice several firms do just lip service to TQM and naturally when it does not bring about the desired change the firm is quick to blame the TQM.

Strategy word comes to business from the armed forces, where during a war, strategies of defeating the enemy are formed. In peacetime, the forces are kept at strategic places to ensure quick deployment when war is declared.

Facing enemy, the commander of the forces needs information on the strength of the enemies forces, number of tanks, armoured vehicles, foot soldiers, aircrafts are with the enemy and their exact deployment locations as also the contour of the terrain. To find this out soldiers are sent on a reconnaissance trip who go behind the enemy lines to gather the information, at the risk of their lives.

In business parlance, it amounts to getting information on competition, business environment of the country and the trade practices followed. Ultimately, the business prospers when the firm surges ahead of competition. This can be achieved by creating Sustainable Competitive Advantage in the firm, which can be done in the following steps:

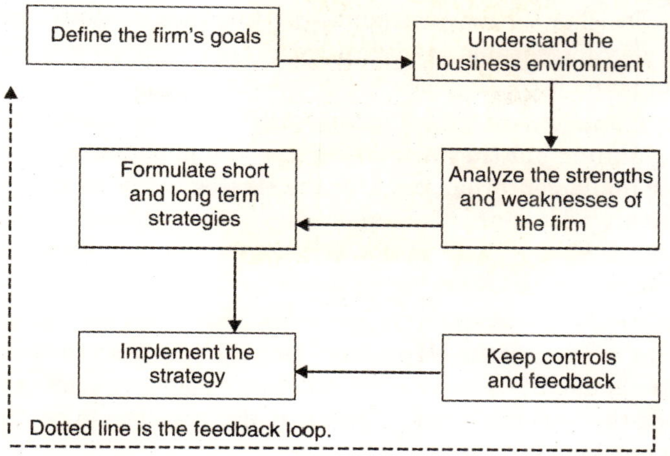

While setting up new retail projects, the project cost takes into account the fund required for any contingencies, which may arise, like increase in cost of the land, building, equipment from the time the project costs were finalized till actual purchase. In a running business contingencies are more of the law rather than exception; hence the need for planning to not only dealing with the contingencies but avoiding them by remaining proactive towards the environmental changes as also changes in the fortunes of the firm.

This above chart is the framework around which the book is being planned for benefiting readers, the students and others planning retail business strategies.

Retail Business Strategy Definition

Business strategy of a firm includes the plans, policies and their implementation in a given timeframe. Plans and policies are converted into action or activities where tasks are assigned to individuals or to teams for achieving specific targets.

Strategy can also be defined as follows:

Strategy is a set of goals and objectives and the firm's policies and plans for achieving the same, correlating with the defined purpose of the firm.

Strategy is the way a firm reacts to its business environment, deploying its resources and marshalling its efforts for achieving its goals.

Strategy is the defining of long and short term goals of the firm and adopting action plans and resource deployment for achieving the same.

Strategy is unified, comprehensive and integrated plan designed for achieving the objectives of the firm.

Strategy relates to the firm's environment, covers both external and internal factors, covers a comprehensive action plan, is flexible to change quickly as per changing environment and is always forward looking.

Peter Drucker the management expert defines strategic management, as planning for foreseeable eventualities as also, perhaps more importantly for those impossible contingencies of which the firm has no prior knowledge

Most management gurus acknowledge the contingent approach to strategic planning but they also insist that the planning must go right up to action or implementation stage for the strategy to be of any effect on the firm. There are a lot of armchair managers in the corporate world; the need today is of the person who is not only a planner but also a doer and a motivator to others to follow his example.

Retail trade management is like managing an ocean liner, except that in a liner the captain of the ship cannot get any help from the outside world. Retail store is usually a busy place with customers swarming it from the town during the working hours,. Therefore, the store has to get the following done after working hours:

1. Cleaning up the place
2. Restocking of the goods
3. Reorganising the merchandising of the goods
4. Placing the signage in right places if they have been displaced
5. Reviewing the pricing strategy and replacing the old price cards with the new ones wherever required
6. Allotment of duties for the next day for the team members
7. Planning for training of the salespersons at lean hours
8. Planning for getting new staff, if required
9. Checking the daily balance sheet, sales, sales returns, cash accruals and sales made on credit. It is necessary to know the reduction in credit with outstanding dues getting paid.
10. Going in depth study of the customer complaints, if any, not just to find out the guilty person but to get into the real cause of the complaint to ensure that it does not recur in the future.

In the retail business of the twenty first century the Stores Managers need to have a lot of imagination, inspiration and emotional bonding with their staff, customers, suppliers, in fact with all their stake- holders to be effective, successful and respected.

The store manager must be able to segregate different job profiles then train persons for each profile, besides a few more to allow and facilitate the members of the team in doing multi-tasking. For this purpose the manager needs to have a good idea of the potential of each person with him. Knowledge about his team will enable the manager to fully and properly utilise the team.

The success of retail comes from its USP-the Unique Selling Preposition. The uniqueness and innovation are the main areas of retail success. The manager has to look into the following for remaining successful:

1. Never oversell to the customer — if the product can be delivered in two weeks time, ask for three weeks and deliver before the promised date to delight the customer.
2. Never oversell even within the organisation, to the owner, or even the salesperson.
3. Know your customers, at least the regulars and call them by their names as you respectfully address them.
4. Surprise your regular customers with something extra once in a while to keep them in good humour always. "Sir, this tie goes well with the shirt you just purchased and it is yours from our side"
5. Direct all your actions only towards achieving your sales and profit targets.
6. Coordinate the sales and service actions for each customer by monitoring the actions of the team members.
7. Keep innovation by the team members as a healthy competition where the best innovator gets recognition as well as some awards.
8. Get the latest low-down on competition with the help of customers, your sales team and competitors sales team.
9. Measure the results regularly with profits, sales volumes, quality and quantity as the yardsticks.

Student's Discussion Points

1. Discuss the importance of ril in FMCG markets.
2. Is product selection a major concern in retail? Discuss.

Management Game

The faculty should divide the class into teams, each consisting of 4 to 5 students. The teams should select a product from the list of FMCG, Consumer Durables and locate a company dealing with it where they have access. Otherwise they can form an imaginary company. Next they should select a name for the company, one product they will like to sell, its features and the customer benefits. They should define their target market segment for the product. Next, they should decide the best way of reaching out to the consumers, the way they want to retail their product, stand-alone single shop, chain stores or shopping malls.

Select a product from either FMCG or Consumer Durable range, select the market coverage area and then decide about the right market segment that the team wants to do business with. Plan Marketing strategies and make P&L Statement for first five years of operations, including sales on yearly basis, profit picture.

Discuss the yearly advertising plan, select the right media, get their rates, try your hand at creating an advertising campaign. Prepare an yearly advertising plan along with its budget.

❍❍❍